FAVRITE
RECIPES

from the

What Hawai'i
LIKES TO EAT™
SERIES

$\mathfrak{Star} \bigstar \mathfrak{Advertiser}$
HONOLULU

What Hawai'i
LIKES TO EAT™
SERIES

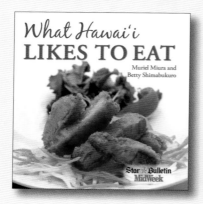

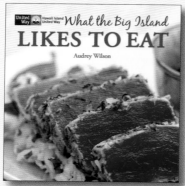

What Hawai'i Likes to Eat (2007)
by Muriel Miura and Betty Shimabukuro

What Hawai'i Likes to Eat Hana Hou (2008)
by Muriel Miura with Galyn Wong

What the Big Island Likes to Eat (2008)
by Audrey Wilson

What Maui Likes to Eat (2010)
by Tylun Pang with Gail Ainsworth

FAVORITE
RECIPES

from the
What Hawai'i
LIKES TO EAT™
SERIES

Muriel Miura
with
Galyn Wong

Food Photography by
Kaz Tanabe

Mutual Publishing

Library of Congress Control Number
available upon request.

ISBN: 978-1939487-51-3

Food photography by Kaz Tanabe,
   unless otherwise noted below
Photos on pg. 13, 19 © Ian Gillespie
Photo on pg. 43 © Douglas Peebles
Photo on pg. 80 © Jim Wilson

Cover design by Jane Gillespie
Design by Courtney Tomasu

First Printing, October 2016
Second Printing, July 2017

Mutual Publishing, LLC
1215 Center Street, Suite 210
Honolulu, Hawai'i 96816
Ph: 808-732-1709 / Fax: 808-734-4094
email: info@mutualpublishing.com
www.mutualpublishing.com

Printed in South Korea

Photos from Dreamstime.com:
pg. i © Andrej Isakovic, pg. v © Sobol100,
pg. vii © Vinaitup, pg. xi © Takt818, pg.
4 © Grigoriev01, pg. 5 © Hlphoto, pg. 23
© Onepony, pg. 31 © Sommail, pg. 34 ©
Devonyu, pg. 35 © Wittybear, pg. 36 ©
Dimabelokoni, pg. 37 © Hin255v, pg. 40, 53,
70 © HandmadePictures, pg. 42 © Sdmix,
pg. 49 © Fortyforks, pg. 51 © Antonio
Muñoz Palomares, pg. 63 © Szefei, pg. 65 ©
Kitzcorner, pg. 66 © Brodogg1313, pg. 87 ©
Artcasta, pg. 89 © Givaga, pg. 93 © Hojo, pg.
98 © Rozmarina, pg. 99 © Volgariver, pg. 105
© Miradrozdowski, pg. 109 © Marysckin, pg.
116 © Ppy2010ha, pg. 122 © Elenadesigner,
pg. 123 © Msk.nina, pg. 133 © Ivan Mateev,
pg. 142 © Maya1313, pg. 143 © Alamourus,
pg. 145 © Ppy2010ha, pg. 156 © Pixbox77, pg.
166 © Dream7904, pg. 167 © Sommail, pg.
170 © Foodio

Star ✪ Advertiser

The *Honolulu Star-Advertiser* knows well and appreciates the popularity of food and cooking in Hawai'i. Every Wednesday, our "Crave" **CookEatDrink** section covers the culinary scene with recipes, chef interviews, restaurant openings, reader queries, and stories. On Sunday, our "Dining Out" section features write-ups and recipes of O'ahu's favorite restaurants.

Cooking is such an integral part of island life that the first thing missed and missed the most, when traveling is local food. Our culinary heritage has been shaped by the ethnicity of Hawai'i's people as well as culinary adaptations from elsewhere.

Several years ago, the question of what does Hawai'i really like to eat was posed to our readers and answered in two books, *What Hawai'i Likes to Eat* and *What Hawai'i Likes to Eat Hana Hou*. These books let everyone know our culinary preferences and how fantastic and unique our local food and cooking are. With these coffee table style books now out-of-stock, we are again teaming up with Mutual Publishing to have in one volume the favorite *What Hawai'i Likes to Eat* dishes.

So, what does Hawai'i like to eat? Everything good, tasty, and relatively easy-to-prepare. The recipes that follow are the favorites of our favorites and show that our island food comes in all varieties, tastes, and flavors which is not surprising, considering how diverse we are as a people.

Dennis Francis
President and publisher,
Honolulu Star-Advertiser
and O'ahu Publications, Inc.

Contents

PŪPŪ

PLATE LUNCH FAVORITES

MAIN DISHES—CHICKEN

MAIN DISHES—PORK

MAIN DISHES—BEEF

MAIN DISHES—SEAFOOD

SALADS, SOUPS, AND SIDES

OMIYAGE

DESSERTS

Acknowledgments

First, mahalo to all those who helped on the initial *What Hawai'i Likes to Eat* books—family members, chefs, home cooks, foodies, and food lovers.

For each volume, many contributed or suggested recipes, food stories, nostalgia, or were involved in the physical production of the book—writers, editors, graphic designers, and proof-readers.

For this title, special thanks to the entire Mutual Staff, particularly Courtney Tomasu, who had to prepare far too many drafts and changes.

Introduction

The *What Hawai'i Likes to Eat* cookbooks began with a simple question—what do islanders most like to eat? What are our favorite foods? The answer is neither singular nor simple. Imagine explaining to someone not from the Islands what constitutes a favorite meal in this distinctive place. There is just so much to choose from.

For *What Hawai'i Likes to Eat* and *What Hawai'i Likes to Eat Hana Hou*, the question was taken to as many people as possible including *Honolulu Star-Advertiser* readers and our network of foodies and experienced eaters. Out of dozens of suggestions, along with our own thoughts, came the recipe collection for *What Hawai'i Likes to Eat* and *What Hawai'i Likes to Eat Hana Hou*. They were later followed by Maui and Big Island editions. The recipes turned out to be varietous—practical, comforting, and refined, just like the people of Hawai'i.

Many of our readers have now asked for just one volume, a best of the best, the favorites of the favorites, and preferably in a smaller size for ease to send or take to friends and family outside of Hawai'i and to use in the kitchen.

Using our same sources, we selected from the volumes in the series, the most favorite and unique recipes. In essence, a volume that is a Hawai'i recipe Hall of Fame. So here they are. Over one hundred and ten recipes that answer the questions what do people in Hawai'i most like to eat, what are our most favorite dishes, and what dishes best identify our culinary tastes and idiosyncrasies.

Not surprising, this hall of fame recipe collection represents all of Hawai'i's ethnic cuisines and all our styles of cooking. Many recipes are old-time favorites handed down through generations, some are contemporary. The collection represents a culinary journey beginning with Hawai'i's melting pot and plantation culinary heritage through to the modern era, when Pacific Rim and the Hawaiian Regional Cuisine became showcases of Hawai'i's cooking, and on to the present day where Hawai'i recipes and food concepts are being exported to the mainland U.S.A.

Food is important in Hawai'i. It defines us not just in time and place, but links us through space and across generations. And it is also especially delicious, or say in Islands: 'ono. These recipes show why.

We dedicate this chapter to audacity—our willingness to take bold risks in food combinations—and to our nerve, sometimes defiant, to adopt a variety of ethnic foods and make them our own. Hawai'i's culinary history is one of acceptance and assimilation, flavorful, enticing, and inspired by the people who have made these islands their home. The recipes collected for this chapter reflect Hawai'i's rich diversity and cultural heritage. Local favorites such as Portuguese Sweet Bread and Fried Saimin, sit alongside new creations such as Kālua Pig BLT Sandwich. These recipes display our willingness to recreate and redefine ourselves while being mindful of the past and how it relates to our present and our future. Throughout, an attempt has been made to capture the essence of aloha in every dish.

ONLY IN HAWAI'I

Loco Moco

Café 100 (Hilo, Island of Hawai'i)

Yield: 1 serving

The absolute mos' famous Big Island dish is loco moco. Teens from the Lincoln Wreckers Athletic Club hung out at a restaurant called the Lincoln Grill, just across from Lincoln Park. Loco moco was sold for twenty-five cents to football players who requested a tasty and filling dish but couldn't afford to pay a lot for it.

Café 100 registered the loco moco name. Nowadays, when we think of loco moco, we might think of Hilo's Café 100, which specializes in the dish. There are usually twenty varieties of loco moco on sale, dishes like: bacon loco; chili loco; mahimahi loco; smoked sausage loco; stew loco; teriyaki loco; oyako loco; hot dog loco; and Spam® loco. If the special of the day is chicken chop suey, the special loco of the day may be chicken chop suey loco.

Café 100 was opened in 1946 by Richard Miyashiro, who named the restaurant to honor his fellow soldiers from the 100th Battalion. The tsunami of 1946 destroyed the restaurant only three months after it was opened. Richard rebuilt his dream restaurant in 1960. Twenty-seven days later it was destroyed in the 1960 tsunami. Café 100 re-opened in 1962 at its present location, 969 Kilauea Avenue.

Loco moco is rice, hamburger, egg, and gravy. It's fairly easy to get the rice and egg right, although the hamburger and gravy are harder.

Gravy stock:

2 pounds beef bones
1 carrot, diced
1 onion, diced
2 stalks celery, diced

Gravy:

¼ cup flour
¼ cup melted butter
1½ cups gravy stock, from stock pot
Salt and pepper to taste

Hamburger patties:

2 pounds lean ground beef
1½ teaspoons salt
¼ teaspoon black pepper
1 egg, beaten
½ cup chopped onion
¼ cup milk
½ cup bread crumbs

Loco moco (1 serving):

1 cup hot cooked rice
1 large fried hamburger patty
1 egg, cooked sunny side up
¼ cup brown gravy

Prepare gravy stock: Good gravy starts with a good stock. Put the diced carrots, onion, and celery in a baking pan. Place the beef bones on top and bake the pan in a 400°F oven for 45 minutes, until the bones are browned. Put the vegetables and bones in a large stock pot, add water to cover, and boil for 1 hour.

Prepare gravy: Whisk the flour into the melted butter over medium heat. Cook until flour and butter form a smooth paste; it should be hot enough to bubble a little. Slowly add the beef stock, stirring constantly so that no lumps form. Simmer for 10 minutes, or until the gravy begins to thicken. Season with salt and pepper to tastes.

Prepare hamburger patties: Combine all ingredients and form into patties.

To assemble loco moco: Put the rice in a large bowl. Put a hamburger patty on top, add the cooked egg, and then pour gravy over the egg.

Sound simple? As you see, it's not.

> *Variation:* **Chili Moco:** *Top the hamburger patty with a serving of your favorite chili (before adding egg and gravy).*

Shoyu Hot Dogs

Chef Hiroshi Fukui

Yield: 4 to 6 servings

Here's a dish so simple that it's actually hard to find a written recipe. You heat the shoyu, you add the hot dog. It's not rocket science. But as with all things, a little attention to technique—in this case, searing the hot dogs, then creating a nice glaze—gives the most humble dish a boost. Chef Hiroshi Fukui, formerly of Hiroshi Eurasion Tapas—known for the most sophisticated and subtle preparations of Euro-Japanese food—provided this formula. After all, who says a chef can't eat simple when he's off-duty?

8 hot dogs
¾ cup sake or water
¼ cup sugar
¼ cup soy sauce

Sear hot dogs in a hot pan; remove. Combine sake, sugar and soy sauce in pan and cook over medium-high heat, stirring to dissolve sugar. Simmer until reduced by half. Return hot dogs to pan and continue cooking, turning hot dogs until they are nicely glazed.

Fish Burger

Yield: About 12 patties

What a difference freshness makes. This fried fish patty, made with fresh tuna, tofu and seasonings puts a fast-food Filet 'o Fish sandwich to shame. Plus, it's designed to be served with rice.

1 pounds aku or 'ahi, minced into fine pieces
1 block tofu, excess water squeezed out
3 tablespoons minced round onion
3 tablespoons minced green onion
½ teaspoon grated fresh ginger
1 teaspoon soy sauce
1 large egg, beaten
Salt and pepper to taste
Canola oil for frying

Combine fish, tofu, round and green onions, ginger, soy sauce, egg, salt, and pepper in large mixing bowl and mix well with hand. Divide into about 4 portions. Return each portion to the cutting board and chop with cleaver until well blended. Form into small patties and fry in hot oil until golden brown. Drain on absorbent paper. Brush patties with your favorite teriyaki or soy sauce, if desired. Serve hot with steamed rice.

Tip: Wrap tofu in cheesecloth and squeeze firmly to remove excess liquid.

'Ahi/Aku Poke Wraps

Yield: 12 rolls

Traditional Hawaiian poke, which means to cut or slice, was prepared with cubed fish flesh which was then flavored with ingredients available in ancient times—sea salt, 'inamona, (roasted, ground kukui nuts). Contemporary poke combines ancient preparation with flavors from the various cultures that have come to Hawai'i since ancient times. It is not uncommon to find wasabi, soy sauce, or won tons in a modern poke dish.

6 sheets bahn trang (dried rice paper wrappers)

Filling:

1 pound 'ahi or aku, cut in ½-inch cubes
½ cup limu kohu (seaweed), blanched and chopped
¼ cup minced green onion
¼ cup Maui onion, thinly sliced
¼ teaspoon sesame oil
2 teaspoons soy sauce
1 teaspoon Hawaiian salt
Hot chili sauce to taste

Wasabi Dipping Sauce:

1 tablespoon wasabi powder
1 tablespoon water
¼ cup soy sauce
½ teaspoon dashi-no-moto
3 tablespoons hot water

To make Filling: Combine all ingredients in medium bowl; toss lightly to mix well. Refrigerate 1 hour before serving.

To make Wasabi Dipping Sauce: Stir together wasabi powder with water; add soy sauce, dashi-no-moto and hot water. Mix well; set aside.

To make Poke Wrap: Dip each bahn trang in a bowl of warm water for a few seconds to soften. Remove; dry with paper towel. Place about 2 to 3 tablespoons of Filling on lower one-third of bahn trang; fold bottom of the wrapper over the Filling. Fold the left and right edges over toward center and roll up tightly into a cylinder, pressing to seal. Repeat until wrappers are all used. Slice each roll in half and serve chilled with Wasabi Dipping Sauce.

Variations:
- Fill bahn trang with shrimp, clams, lobster, an assortment of seafoods instead of fish.
- Combine sushi rice with vegetables and seafood of choice.
- Combine steamed rice with teriyaki meat and vegetables of choice.

Note: *Bahn trang (dried rice paper wrappers) are sold in Asian stores or in the oriental/Asian food section of supermarkets in plastic packets containing about 10 or more wrappers, which are about 8 to 10 inches in diameter.*

Teriyaki Chicken Wings

Yield: About 6 servings

This recipe fills me with nostalgia making my thoughts wander back to small kid time. I wonder how many chickens my cousin sold from his Chicken Cradle stall at Oahu Market until very recently when he retired. I wonder how many eggs my cousins packed on the farm they had at one time on Halemaumau Road? I wonder how many chicks were hatched in their hatchery? —MURIEL MIURA

2 pounds chicken wings
6 to 8 Japanese taro (dasheen)
1 stalk green onion, chopped

Teriyaki Sauce:

⅔ cup soy sauce
½ cup brown sugar, packed
¼ cup sake (rice wine)
½ teaspoon fresh grated ginger root

Cut tips off chicken wings. Peel taro; cut into quarters or halves. Combine Teriyaki Sauce ingredients; heat to dissolve sugar. Add chicken and taro; cover and bring to a boil over medium heat. Turn heat down to low and simmer for 30 to 45 minutes, stirring occasionally. Add green onion; turn heat off. Delicious with hot, steamed rice.

Variation: ***Teriyaki Chicken:*** *Cook chicken thighs or other chicken parts in Teriyaki Sauce.*

Tsukudani Spam® Musubi

Yield: 40 musubi

Of course, no one really needs a recipe for Spam® Musubi. You press a scoop of rice into the mold, top with a slice of luncheon meat, and wrap it all in a half-sheet of nori. Continue until you run out of one ingredient or another.

But there's always a way to fancy things up. This version is based on one pioneered by David Hisashima, a courtroom deputy at U.S. District Court who made it up for office potlucks. His secret: nori paste, or tsukudani, spread between Spam® and rice. You will need an acrylic musubi-making mold, sold at drugstores and many supermarkets.

> **2 cans (12 oz. size) Spam®, cut into 20 slices**
> **1 cup prepared teriyaki sauce**
> **7½ cups cooked rice**
> **10 sheets sushi nori (seaweed), cut in half**
> **1½ bottles (1.5-oz. size) furikake**
> **1 jar (3.3 oz.) tsukudani nori (flavored seaweed paste)**

Fry Spam® until lightly browned. Brush with teriyaki sauce; set aside. Mix rice with furikake.

Lay a piece of nori flat on work surface. Center a Spam® musubi mold over nori.

Fill mold half-way with rice. Spread paste over rice and top with Spam®. Press mixture into mold. Fill mold with more rice; press again. Fold nori over Spam® and seal. Cool; cut musubi in half.

Tips:

~ *Keep the nori dry, but your utensils moist. Water keeps rice from sticking to your mold, rice scoop and knife. But if the nori gets wet it will shrivel and shrink. Use some water, though, to seal the nori once it's wrapped around the rice.*

~ *If you make a lot of Spam® musubi, invest in a double-wide mold. You can make two at a time, and you don't have to cut the nori in half.*

(continued on page 12)

Musubi Variations

Furikake Spam® Musubi:

Sprinkle rice with furikake before placing luncheon meat in mold.

Spam® Omelette:

Scramble 2 to 3 large eggs with 1 teaspoon soy sauce. Cook in hot oil in skillet until well done; slice to fit musubi mold. Sprinkle furikake over rice before topping with egg, followed by slice of Spam®.

Teri-Spam®:

Cook Spam® slices in 3 tablespoons each of soy sauce, mirin, and sugar for 1 to 2 minutes. Drain well before making musubi.

Teri-Chicken:

Cook thin slices of boneless chicken breast in ½ cup each of soy sauce, mirin, and sugar for 2 to 3 minutes or until chicken is cooked through; drain. Substitute chicken for luncheon meat.

Teri-Beef:

Cook thin slices of lean beef in ¼ cup each of soy sauce, mirin, and sugar for 1 to 2 minutes or until beef is cooked; drain. Substitute teri-beef for luncheon meat.

Korean-Style:

Toss cooked rice with 1 teaspoon toasted sesame seeds and 1 tablespoon sesame-chili oil; mix well. Place well-drained chopped cabbage kim chee (Korean pickle) on rice before placing Spam® or teri beef on rice.

Easy Boiled Peanuts

Yield: 2 pounds

Back in the good ol' days, football and baseball games were played at the Honolulu Stadium, located at the corner of Isenberg and South King Streets. Back then, spectators didn't have the variety of concession choices offered at modern stadiums. Still there was good eating to be had. There were the usual snacks—popcorn, soda, ice cream, chips, shaved ice, candy bars, hot dogs, and hamburgers—but, before entering the stadium, nearly everyone stopped to buy boiled peanuts from the "Peanut Lady," who sold them in brown paper bags outside the main gate. —MURIEL MIURA

2 pounds raw peanuts in shell
½ cup Hawaiian salt
2 to 3 whole star anise
1 tablespoon sugar

Place peanuts in a large pot and cover with water. Add salt, star anise and sugar. Bring to a boil, cover, and simmer for 1 to 1½ hours, stirring occasionally, or until peanuts are tender but firm. Add more water as necessary to keep peanuts covered with water. Adjust seasoning as necessary. Cool and drain. Will keep in refrigerator 2 to 3 days.

Oxtail Stew

Yield: About 4 to 6 servings

During the 1960s I was part owner of a coffee shop situated in a bowling alley on the windward side of O'ahu. The coffee shop offered a typical breakfast menu of eggs with ham, bacon or luncheon meat and pancakes. For lunch and dinner, hamburger steak with gravy, roast pork or chicken, rarely roast beef (too expensive), chili with hotdog, beef stew or curry were offered. Every so often, we featured Oxtail Stew on the menu. Until then, I had never tasted that dish but I eventually grew to love it.

Over the years, bowling alley menus have advanced far beyond the simple fare we were offering at our coffee shop. I've seen some restaurants offer such gourmet items as furikake salmon and garlic shrimp. Fancy! —Muriel Miura

4 to 5 pounds oxtail, disjointed and fat removed
1 cup flour
½ cup salad oil
2 medium onions, wedged
1 clove garlic, chopped
5 cups water (more if necessary)
2 bay leaves
1½ teaspoons salt
¼ teaspoon pepper
2 cans (8 oz. each) tomato sauce
1 can (10¾ oz.) can condensed tomato soup
4 small carrots, cut into 1-inch pieces
4 small potatoes, pared and quartered
1 cup sliced celery
Flour-water mixture for thickening, optional

Dredge oxtails in flour; brown lightly in large pot on all sides in hot oil. Add onions and garlic; brown lightly. Add water and bay leaves; bring to a boil; cover and simmer 1½ to 2 hours or until oxtails are tender. Add remaining ingredients; simmer additional 30 minutes or until vegetables are done. Thicken with flour-water paste, if desired. Adjust taste as necessary.

Saimin

Yield: 2 to 3 servings

Saimin represents a third-stage evolution. In the beginning, there was mein—Chinese noodles. Then came the Japanese adaptation—ramen. In Hawai'i, the chewy noodles in broth became saimin.

The first saimin recipes show up in local cookbooks in the 1930s; the first vendors were Japanese immigrants who sold their noodles from pushcarts, often set up outside gas stations. Garnished with char siu, green onion, and maybe a few strips of fried egg, saimin is for many of us a warm bowl of slurpy comfort.

Saimin Noodles

2 cups flour
½ teaspoon salt
4 eggs
2 teaspoons water (if needed)
5 tablespoons cornstarch

Mix flour and salt together. Add unbeaten eggs and work well into flour; add water, 1 teaspoon at a time. Sprinkle work surface with 1 tablespoon cornstarch; roll dough paper thin. Sprinkle dough with a layer of cornstarch and roll up on rolling pin. Press with the palms of the hands. Remove from rolling pin. Repeat process 3 or 4 times, using all of the cornstarch. Remove from rolling pin; fold and cut into fine strips or use noodle-making machine, following manufacturer's instructions.

Cook noodles in boiling water to cover 1 to 2 minutes or until done; drain and rinse with hot water. Place noodles in individual bowls; ladle broth over noodles and garnish with desired condiments.

Saimin Dashi

2 quarts water
½ cup dried shrimps
1 piece (2 x 6-inch) dashi konbu
2 teaspoons salt
2 teaspoons soy sauce
½ teaspoon MSG, optional

Garnishes:

Kamaboko slices
Luncheon meat, cut into strips
Char siu, cut into slices or strips
Fried egg strips
Minced green onion

Combine water with dried shrimps and konbu. Bring water to a boil; remove konbu and simmer over low heat for 20 to 30 minutes. Discard shrimp. Add remaining seasonings; adjust taste as necessary. Pour over cooked noodles; garnish with desired condiments.

Taro Stew

Yield: 6 servings

Often referred to as paniolo (cowboy) stew, the Hawaiian taro is used in this soup in place of potatoes. This stew will serve as a hearty treat to all the rough and tumble cowpokes in your house! —MURIEL MIURA

¼ cup flour
¾ teaspoon salt
⅛ teaspoon pepper
2 pounds boneless stewing beef
2 tablespoons canola oil
1 large onion, sliced
1 clove garlic, crushed
1 small piece fresh ginger, crushed
1 Hawaiian red pepper, seeded and minced
½ teaspoon peppercorns
5 to 6 cups water
2 large carrots, peeled and cut into 1-inch pieces
2 pounds taro, peeled and cut into 1-inch pieces
1 cup chopped green onions
1 teaspoon Hawaiian salt
Poi to thicken, optional

Combine flour, salt and pepper; dredge beef in flour mixture.

In a large pot, brown beef in hot oil. Stir in onion, garlic, ginger, red pepper and peppercorns. Add water; bring to a boil and cover; simmer for 1½ to 2 hours or until beef is tender. Add carrots and taro; cover and simmer additional 30 to 40 minutes. Add green onions and salt just before serving. Adjust seasoning as necessary. Thicken stew to desired consistency with poi, if used.

Fried Saimin
(Yaki Ramen)

Yield: 4 to 6 servings

This fast and simple dish is perfect for those times when unexpected company drops by or when the kids need a quick snack. —MURIEL MIURA

½ cup chicken or pork, slivered
1 tablespoon salad oil
6 shrimp, cleaned and minced
⅓ cup bamboo shoots, sliced
½ cup celery, sliced diagonally
½ cup green onion, cut in 1-inch lengths
½ pound bean sprouts, washed and drained
1 tablespoon toasted sesame seeds
1 pound fresh cooked ramen

Seasonings:

2 teaspoons soy sauce
¼ cup chicken broth
1 teaspoon salt

Garnishes:

2 tablespoons toasted sesame seeds
¼ cup minced green onion
Chinese parsley sprigs

Stir-fry chicken or pork in hot oil for 2 minutes. Add shrimp, stir-fry additional minute. Add vegetables, noodles and seasonings; stir-fry 1 minute to heat through. Garnish with sesame seeds, green onions and Chinese parsley.

Variations: Cooked soba, udon or chuka soba (chow mein) may be substituted for ramen.

Kālua Pig BLT Sandwich

The Pineapple Room, Macy's Ala Moana

Yield: 4 servings

Kālua pig is a local favorite. The dish is traditionally prepared in an imu, or underground oven. The pig can take hours to cook. When the pork is at last fully cooked it is raised from the imu to take its place as the delicious centerpiece of any Hawaiian lū'au or local gathering.

Chef Alan Wong has put his own spin on this local classic. Served on an onion bun with Caesar Salad, the Kālua Pig BLT has become one of the most popular dishes at Alan Wong's Pineapple Room located on the top floor of Macy's Ala Moana. It is truly an awesome sandwich and one that you'll just have to try!

¾ pound oven kālua pig
1 large tomato, cut 4 thin
   slices
2 tablespoons minced onion
1 tablespoon minced green
   onion
2 tablespoons Boursin cheese

¼ cup mayonnaise
4 onion buns, split
4 slices cooked thick bacon,
   cut into thirds
4 leaves lettuce, washed and
   dried (optional)

Heat kālua pig in small skillet only until heated through; set aside. Save 4 slices tomato on the side; mince remaining tomato and combine with minced onion and green onion in small bowl; mix well. In small dish, mix together Boursin cheese and mayonnaise; spread tops and bottoms of buns with mixture. Place about 3 ounces kālua pig on each bottom half of buns then top with minced tomato-onion mixture, bacon, slice of tomato and lettuce if used. Top with remaining half of bun.

The traditional kālua pig is a whole pig prepared in an underground oven, or imu. It takes hours to cook the pork and when it is done to perfection, it is raised from the imu in the midst of a ceremony of prayer, music and dancing at a Hawaiian lū'au. Today, kālua pig, a Hawaiian favorite is often prepared in the kitchen using pork butt or shoulder.

If kālua pig in not available, oven-smoke and braise pork roast in a shallow pan by combining 1½ teaspoons liquid smoke with about 3 cups of chicken broth and placing the pork roast in the broth to cook for 3 to 3½ hours or until fork-tender. Shred cooked pork using two forks and keep in the broth until ready to use. Freeze unused smoked pork for later use.

Variations: Smoked pork, chicken, turkey or duck may be substituted for kālua pig.

Portuguese Sweet Bread

Yield: 7 rolls per pan

If you have a stand mixer with a dough hook, you will find this bread easy to make. Most of the work consists of waiting for the dough to rise.

Experienced bakers will tell you to let the rolls cool before breaking them open, buttering, and eating them. The bread continues cooking, with residual heat, even after you take it out of the oven. If you eat the bread straight out of the oven, it may still be a little gummy in the center. However, even experienced bakers have difficulty restraining themselves when the bread smells and tastes SO GOOD!

½ cup warm but not hot water
1¼ cups evaporated milk
2¼ teaspoons (1 package) dry yeast
4 tablespoons butter, melted
1 large egg, beaten
½ cup sugar
1½ teaspoons salt
4 cups all-purpose flour

For the egg wash:

1 egg
2 tablespoons milk

Mix the water, evaporated milk, and yeast in the bowl of your stand mixer. You can use the paddle attachment for this first step. (If you don't have a mixer, beat well with a spoon.)

Melt the butter and beat the egg. Switch to the dough hook attachment for the mixer. Add the melted butter, egg, sugar, salt, and flour to the yeast and mix to combine.

Knead the dough with the dough hook until the dough is evenly mixed, soft, and pliable (or knead by hand if you don't have a stand mixer with a dough hook). The kneading may take 5 or 6 minutes with a mixer, as long as 10 by hand. The dough should collect in a lump while you are kneading it. If the dough is too sticky and clings to the sides of the bowl, add a little extra flour.

Lift the dough out of the mixing bowl, pour a little cooking oil into the bowl, and roll the ball of dough around in the oil. It should not stick to the walls of the bowl. It is OK if there are still some streaks of dried dough on the sides of the bowl; you can wash those out later.

Cover the bowl with a lid, a cloth, or a piece of plastic wrap. Put the bowl in a warm place, and let the dough rise until doubled. This will usually take about 1 hour, but if your kitchen is chilly, this may take longer.

Roll the dough into a long snake and divide it into 7 equal pieces. Roll the pieces into balls.

Oil a 10-inch diameter round pan. Arrange 6 of the dough balls around the edge of the pan and put 1 in the center. Cover the pan and let the dough rise again. It should rise for about 1 hour, or until the dough still bounces back when poked lightly with a finger. (If it doesn't bounce back, it is over-risen and won't have much oven spring.)

Before the dough has finished rising, preheat the oven to 350°F.

Beat the egg for the egg wash and mix it with the milk. Gently brush the egg wash over the top of the rolls. Careful; you don't want to deflate the rolls. Bake at 350°F for 30 to 40 minutes. Turn the rolls out of the pan and cool them on a wire rack.

Chantilly Cake

Yield: 8 to 10 servings

Classic French chantilly is sweetened whipped cream with nuts or fruit sometimes added. In Hawai'i it's a golden, buttery frosting. This recipe was developed in the Honolulu Gas Company's test kitchen in the '60s, when the Chantilly Cake from Liliha Bakery was becoming all the rage. It was featured in the "Blue Flame" cooking classes and was frequently requested during the pre-Internet days when recipes could be obtained by phone from home economists at the public utilities and the state extension services. —MURIEL MIURA

Cake:

2 eggs, separated
1½ cups sugar
1¾ cups cake flour
¾ teaspoon baking soda
1 teaspoon salt
⅓ cup vegetable oil
1 cup buttermilk
2 squares (2 oz. each) sweet
  baking chocolate, melted

Make a meringue by beating egg whites until frothy; gradually beat in ½ cup of the sugar. Continue beating until very stiff and glossy. Set aside.

Sift together remaining sugar, flour, baking soda, and salt. Make a well in the center of the flour mixture; add oil and half of the buttermilk. Beat 1 minute, medium speed on mixer or 150 vigorous strokes by hand. Add remaining buttermilk, egg yolks and chocolate. Beat 1 additional minute. Fold in meringue. Pour into 2 greased and floured 9-inch layer pans. Bake at 350°F for 30 to 35 minutes or until wooden pick inserted comes out clean. Cool. Spread Cream Filling between layers. Frost sides and top with Pecan Frosting.

Cream Filling

Yield: 1 cup

¼ cup sugar
⅛ teaspoon salt
1¼ tablespoons cornstarch
1 egg, slightly beaten
1 cup milk, scalded
½ tablespoon butter
½ teaspoon vanilla

Combine first three ingredients; add egg, stirring until well blended. Stir in milk slowly and cook over low heat, stirring constantly, until mixture comes to a boil and thickens. Add butter and vanilla; stir well. Cool. Spread between layers.

Butter Pecan Frosting

Yield: Frosting for 9-inch layer cake

1½ cups evaporated milk (do not dilute)
1½ cups sugar
4 egg yolks
¾ cup butter or margarine
1½ teaspoons vanilla
1½ cups chopped pecans or nuts of choice

Combine all ingredients except pecans in saucepan. Cook over low heat or double boiler, stirring constantly, for about 12 minutes or until mixture thickens. Add pecans; beat until frosting is thick enough to spread.

Mai Tai Chiffon Pie

Yield: 8 servings

A sweet rum drink meaning "good" or "out of this world," the Mai Tai has become synonymous with Hawai'i. At your next get-together, surprise your guests with slices of this exotic pie topped with cherries, mint and maybe even an orchid blossom or two atop the whipped cream.
—MURIEL MIURA

- 1 tablespoon unflavored gelatin
- ¼ cup water
- 3 eggs, separated
- ½ cup sugar
- ½ teaspoon salt
- 3 tablespoons liquid Mai Tai mix
- ¼ cup blended Mai Tai rum
- 1¼ teaspoons lemon zest
- 2 to 3 drops red food coloring
- ⅓ cup sugar
- 9-inch baked pie shell

Garnishes:

- 1 cup sweetened whipped cream
- 6 candied or maraschino cherries, chopped
- Sprig of mint
- Vanda or dendrobium orchid blossoms, optional

Soften gelatin with water. Beat egg yolks until thickened in saucepan. Blend in the ½ cup sugar, salt and Mai Tai mix; cook over low heat, stirring constantly, until mixture thickens. Remove from heat; add softened gelatin and stir until gelatin is thoroughly dissolved. Stir in rum, lemon zest and food coloring; chill until mixture begins to thicken. Beat egg whites until soft peaks form; gradually add the ⅓ cup sugar beating until stiff peaks form. Gently fold the chilled mixture into the egg whites. Pour into baked pie shell and chill until firm, about 2 hours. Top with sweetened whipped cream; garnish with cherries, mint and orchid.

*Tip: **Mai Tai Mix:** ⅓ ounce oregeat syrup, ⅓ ounce Rock Candy syrup and ⅓ ounce orange curacao (Bols).*

Chocolate Dream Cake

Yield: 8 to 10 servings

Look up "chocolate dream cake" in a mainstream cookbook and you'll find a rich chocolate cake with all manner of mix-ins, from nuts to cherry pie filling. In Hawai'i, though, a chocolate dream cake is a light chiffon with a whipped cream frosting.

2 eggs, separated	⅓ cup vegetable oil
1½ cups sugar	1 cup buttermilk
1¾ cups cake flour	2 squares (2 oz. each)
¾ teaspoon baking soda	unsweetened baking
1 teaspoon salt	chocolate, melted

Beat egg whites until frothy. Gradually beat in ½ cup of the sugar. Continue beating until very stiff and glossy. Set aside.

Sift together remaining sugar, flour, baking soda, and salt. Make a well in the center of the flour mixture; add oil and half of the buttermilk. Beat 1 minute, medium speed on mixer or 150 vigorous strokes by hand. Add remaining buttermilk, egg yolks and chocolate. Beat 1 additional minute. Fold in beaten egg whites. Pour into 2 greased and floured 9-inch layer pans. Bake at 350°F for 30 to 35 minutes or until wooden pick inserted comes out clean. Set aside; cool.

Filling and Frosting:

2 cups whipping cream, chilled
⅓ cup sugar
¼ teaspoon vanilla extract, optional
Chocolate curls

For Filling and Frosting, beat whipping cream in a large chilled bowl with mixer at high speed until soft peaks form. Gradually add sugar and vanilla, if used; beat until stiff peaks form. Cover with plastic wrap; refrigerate until ready to use.

To assemble, split each cake layer in half horizontally. Place one split cake layer on serving plate. Spread whipped topping on top; repeat with remaining layers and whipped topping saving enough to frost sides and top of cake. Sprinkle top and sides with chocolate shavings and curls, pushing curls slightly into topping. Refrigerate until ready to serve.

Tips:

Chocolate Curls: *Draw vegetable peeler along underside or side of slightly warm (room temperature may be fine on a hot day) chocolate. Curl will form naturally. Lift curl with wooden pick onto waxed paper covered tray or dish.*

Chocolate Shavings: *Drag a vegetable peeler across a square of chocolate in short quick strokes.*

Grated Chocolate: *Rub chocolate across the rough surface of a grater, letting the pieces fall onto waxed paper. Size of grater holes will determine the size of the chocolate pieces.*

In the early stages of compiling the original *What Hawaii Likes to Eat* book, hours were spent sifting through favorite recipes, old and new. Nostalgia exacted a great pull on the taste buds. Many of the dishes considered evoked memories not just of taste but also of bygone times, places, and people—from the old Third Floor Restaurant to the even older Stewart's Pharmacy.

Some recipes came from Betty Shimabukuro's popular weekly recipe column "By Request" that has appeared in *The Honolulu Star Bulletin* and now the *Honolulu Star-Advertiser*. Often the name of a restaurant is forgotten, just that it was on the corner of such-and-such street near such and such place, and it served the best scones/oxtail soup/roast chicken/hamburger stew, anywhere, anytime. Here are the absolute best memory lane recipes. Some of these dishes are stunners perfect for special celebrations; others are simple, everyday favorites.

UNFORGETTABLE

Taro Biscuits

Napua Stevens

Yield: 1 Dozen

Taro has become the basis for quite a few baked good in recent years. The key reason, although few bakers probably realize it, is that taro is high in a substance called soluble gum, which makes baked goods seem rich even if they don't contain much fat. These Taro Biscuits, courtesy of entertainer Napua Stevens, are a favorite from the 1960s.

1 cup cooked taro, mashed
¼ cup shortening
1½ cups flour
3 teaspoons baking powder
2 teaspoons sugar
½ teaspoon salt
1 egg, beaten
¼ cup milk

Combine taro and shortening; blend well then add the dry ingredients. Add the egg and milk; stir to combine then knead on lightly floured board. Pat to ½-inch thickness, cut with biscuit cutter then place biscuits about 1-inch apart on lightly greased cookie sheet. Bake at 425°F for 15 minutes or until golden brown. 'Ono with butter and guava or liliko'i preserve.

Summer 'Ahi Tartare

Sam Choy's Kaloko Restaurant

Yield: 6 servings

Sam Choy and his sister, Claire Wai Sun Choy, opened the Kaloko Restaurant in 1991. It was a favorite with both locals and tourists. Unfortunately, the restaurant has since closed down.

Fresh-caught fish was always available at the Kaloko. The restaurant sold one thousand pounds of fried marlin poke every week. They also sold mahimahi lū'au, steamed opah, weke 'ula, and 'ōpakapaka.

When the cooks cleaned the 'ahi and cut fillets, they scraped the bones to make this 'ahi tartare.

1 pound very fresh 'ahi or yellowfin tuna
¼ cup minced sweet onion
2½ tablespoons lemon juice (juice of 1 lemon, approximately)
2 tablespoons chopped cilantro
1 tablespoon minced fresh ginger
1 tablespoon soy sauce
1 teaspoon olive oil
1 teaspoon sesame oil
1½ teaspoons grated fresh horseradish
½ teaspoon prepared stone-ground mustard
Pinch of red chili pepper flakes
Salt and white pepper to taste

Cut the 'ahi into 1-inch cubes. Combine all ingredients in a food processor and do 6 short pulses until the fish reaches the texture you prefer. Do NOT purée the mixture.

If you don't have a processor, use a sharp knife to mince the 'ahi into ¼-inch cubes. Combine the chopped 'ahi with the other ingredients.

Serve with toast points, crackers, or field greens.

Filet Mignon with Black Bean Sauce

Inn of the 6th Happiness

Yield: 2 Servings

Inn of the 6th Happiness was a Chinese restaurant with high aims; witness this filet mignon dish that combined black bean sauce in a basic stir-fry presentation.

- **2 bell peppers, seeded and shredded**
- **2 tablespoons salad oil**
- **5 ounces filet mignon, cut into strips**
- **1 teaspoon soy sauce**
- **1 teaspoon sugar**
- **Pinch of salt**
- **1 teaspoon mixture of minced garlic and mashed black beans**
- **1 teaspoon cornstarch**
- **1 teaspoon water**

Sauté bell pepper in hot oil 1 to 2 minutes. Add filet mignon and stir-fry 30 seconds; stir in soy sauce, sugar, salt and garlic-black beans mixture. Combine cornstarch with water to make paste and add to mixture; cook until gravy is thickened.

Serve with hot steamed rice.

Teriyaki Beef

May Goya, May's Fountain

Yield: 6 servings

May Goya started her restaurant, May's Fountain, after the tsunami of 1946. The restaurant was destroyed in the tsunami of 1960, and May re-opened on the corner of Ponahawai and Punahoa streets. This popular lunch spot closed in 1977.

Here is May's recipe for teriyaki beef.

1½ pounds teriyaki meat, sliced very thin

Marinade:

1¼ cups brown or white sugar
1¼ cups soy sauce
1 tablespoon salad oil
1 clove garlic, crushed
2 teaspoons crushed ginger

Mix soy sauce, sugar, oil, garlic, and ginger in a bowl. Add the beef, soak overnight. Charcoal grill or pan fry. When pan frying, cook until the sauce gets thick.

Chicken Pineapple

La Ronde Restaurants, Inc

Yield: 2 to 4 Servings

The La Ronde, the rotating restaurant atop the Ala Moana Building, was the ultimate date restaurant. A place you'd go when you had enough money saved to treat that someone special to a fabulous view and a meticulously served meal. Perhaps you'd share this dish of chicken with a curried pineapple sauce.

> 4 pieces boneless chicken breasts
> 1 egg, beaten
> ½ cup bread crumbs
> ½ cup salad oil for frying
>
> Pineapple Sauce:
>
> 1 can (8 oz.) pineapple juice
> 1 cup sugar
> 2 teaspoons curry powder
> Juice of ½ lemon
> 1 tablespoon cornstarch

Dip chicken in egg; dredge in bread crumbs. Pan fry in hot oil until golden brown; drain on absorbent paper. Place in baking dish.

Mix together Pineapple Sauce ingredients and pour over chicken. Bake at 350°F for 30 minutes.

Sesame Chicken Orientale

La Mancha Restaurant

Yield: 4 to 5 servings

A simple recipe found in our archives, this dish offers a novel variation on teriyaki chicken. This recipe is relatively easy to make and uses readily available ingredients, but the flavor is complex and satisfying.
—MURIEL MIURA

- 2 pounds boneless chicken breasts
- 1 tablespoon sherry
- ½ cup soy sauce
- 1 tablespoon sesame oil
- 1 tablespoon toasted sesame seeds
- ½ cup flour
- 1 cup cornstarch
- 6 tablespoons brown sugar
- 3 large eggs
- 3 teaspoons minced garlic
- 2 teaspoons minced shallots
- 2 stalks green onion, minced
- 2 teaspoons grated fresh ginger

Combine all ingredients, except chicken, in large bowl and mix thoroughly. Place the chicken in the batter making sure that each piece is completely coated; cover the bowl and refrigerate overnight or at least 8 hours. Deep-fry in oil heated to 350 to 375°F until golden brown on both sides and done. Drain on absorbent paper and serve immediately.

Bread Pudding

Surf Room, Royal Hawaiian Hotel

Yield: About 16 servings

Island residents are crazy about bread pudding, and restaurants offer countless versions in all manner of fancy flavors and presentations. The Surf Room, an island institution in the Royal Hawaiian Hotel, serves a classic version that has been popular for decades.

15 eggs
1 cup + 3 tablespoons sugar
1½ quarts milk
½ quart heavy whipping cream
6 tablespoons vanilla extract
1 long loaf French bread
¾ cup golden raisins

Vanilla Sauce:

1 quart heavy cream
1 cup sugar
6 egg yolks
1 tablespoon vanilla extract

Mix eggs and sugar in a mixing bowl at low speed for 3 minutes. Add milk, cream and vanilla, continuing to mix for 4 minutes; strain and set aside.

Slice bread and pack into 20 x 12-inch baking pans as tightly as possible. Sprinkle raisins on top; pour egg-milk mixture over to fill pan ¼ of its height and let soak 5 minutes. Push bread down; add remaining liquid and let stand 10 minutes. Cover with lightly greased foil and place bread pudding pan inside a larger baking pan. Add water between pans until liquid almost reaches to top. Bake at 400°F for about 90 minutes or until golden brown. Serve with Vanilla Sauce.

Preparing Vanilla Sauce: While bread pudding is baking, prepare Vanilla Sauce by heating heavy cream in saucepan. Combine sugar, yolks, and vanilla in stainless steel mixing bowl; mix well. After cream comes to a boil, slowly add to the egg mixture, whipping constantly.

Return egg-cream mixture to saucepan and place back on heat, stirring constantly. When the mixture comes to a boil, remove pan from heat, return mixture to the stainless steel bowl, and place in an ice bath. Continue stirring until temperature reaches about 75°F; refrigerate until ready to use. Sauce will thicken as it cools; add milk to adjust to desired consistency.

Quick substitute: Instead of 1 cup whole milk, use ½ cup evaporated milk plus ½ cup water or 1 cup water plus ⅓ cup nonfat dry milk powder.

Banana Muffins

Tahitian Lanai

Yield: 4 Dozen

The Tahitian Lanai was 40 years old when it closed in 1997, one of the last relics of Old Waikīkī. The restaurant was known for its continental cuisine, delivered with a bit of a Polynesian twist, but also for its breakfast and brunch items. These muffins are a classic.

> 1½ cups butter or margarine
> 2 cups sugar
> 6 eggs, beaten
> 1 cup mashed banana
> ¼ teaspoon vanilla
> ¼ teaspoon banana flavoring
> 4 cups cake flour
> 1½ teaspoons baking soda
> ¼ teaspoon salt

Cream together butter or margarine and sugar until light and fluffy. Add beaten eggs, mashed banana, vanilla, and banana flavoring. Mix well. Sift the flour, baking soda, and salt together 3 times. Add to banana mixture. Do not over-mix. Turn into greased or lined muffin cups and bake at 350°F for 20 minutes or until golden brown.

Sky High Coconut Cream Pie

The Willows

Yield: 8 to 10 servings

The garden setting of the Willows is legendary, and so is this pie, known for its tall, billowing topping of meringue. The restaurant was shut down for many years, during which residents went through withdrawal. Since reopening in 1999, this famous pie is still being served.

2 cups milk
½ cup sugar
¼ cup grated fresh coconut
5 tablespoons cornstarch
4 egg yolks
1 tablespoon butter
Pinch of salt
Vanilla extract to taste
1 (9-inch) baked pie shell

Meringue:

4 to 6 egg whites
Approximately 1 tablespoon sugar for each egg white
Grated fresh coconut

Put milk, sugar, salt, and coconut in saucepan over medium heat and cook until it comes to near boil; mix cornstarch and egg yolks together with a little water and add to milk mixture, stirring continually until thickened over low heat; add butter, salt and vanilla. Stir, cool and pour into baked and cooled pie shell. Top with meringue.

To prepare meringue, beat egg whites until stiff but not dry; add sugar gradually, beating continuously. Spread over cooled filling, sealing to edges of pastry. Sprinkle coconut over top. Brown in 400°F oven.

Pūpū—Hawaiian for appetizers, or finger food—are some of the easiest dishes to make and to share. No party platter or home buffet is complete without an array of pūpūs served. They are the forever favorites at potlucks. Pūpūs are as diverse as Hawai'i's vast array of culinary ingredients and flavors and reflect contributions from all of Hawai'i's ethnic and social groups. Poke recipes are particularly popular now showing up wherever food is served or sold.

PŪPŪ

'Ahi Poke Hawaiian-Style

Chef Sam Choy

Yield: 6 to 8 as an appetizer

This dish typifies contemporary Hawaiian-style poke. It blends traditional Hawaiian ingredients ('ahi, Hawaiian salt, limu kohu) with Asian touches (soy sauce, sesame oil) to create a multi-cultural blend of flavors. I've always maintained that Hawai'i is at the crossroads of the culinary universe; this simple but tasty dish is case in point. And the sweet Maui onion gives it just the right taste.

1 pound sashimi-grade 'ahi, cut into ¾-inch dice
1 medium-sized tomato, trimmed and cut into ¼-inch dice
½ cup Maui onion, peeled and chopped
2 tablespoons soy sauce
1 teaspoon sesame oil
½ teaspoon granulated sugar
½ teaspoon red chili pepper flakes
   OR 1 Hawaiian chili pepper, trimmed and minced
2 tablespoons green onion, chopped, for garnish

Combine the 'ahi, tomato, onion, soy sauce, sesame oil, sugar, and the red chili pepper flakes or minced chili pepper. Mix well. Allow flavors to blend for 1 hour before serving. Garnish with the chopped green onion before serving.

Poke 'Ahi/Aku

Yield: 6 servings

Traditional Hawaiian-style poke was made with the flavorings at hand in ancient times: sea salt and 'inamona, or roasted, ground kukui nuts. The word "poke" means to slice or cut, reflective of the small pieces of fish used. Modern-day poke comes in countless varieties, reflecting immigrant influences, mainly soy sauce and sesame oil.

1 pound 'ahi or aku, cut in ½-inch cubes
½ cup limu kohu (seaweed), blanched and chopped
1 tablespoon Hawaiian (rock) salt
1 Hawaiian red chili pepper, seeded and minced
1½ teaspoons 'inamona (ground, roasted kukui nut)

Combine all ingredients; toss to mix well. Chill before serving.

World Famous Fried Marlin Poke

Chef Sam Choy

Yield: 4 servings

Through his annual Poke Festival, Sam Choy has raised the profile of the traditional island dish and pushed the envelope of what can be considered poke. No longer restricted to a rough mixture of raw cubes of fish, the definition of poke has widened to include tofu, other seafoods, even cooked fish. Fried poke is actually pan-seared, so the fish is still raw on the inside. It's tossed with typical poke ingredients of onions, soy sauce and sesame oil, but Sam also adds some raw veggies.

20 ounces fresh raw marlin
4 teaspoons soy sauce
1 cup chopped onion
4 teaspoons chopped green onions
1 cup rinsed and chopped ogo seaweed
4 teaspoons sesame oil
1 tablespoon vegetable oil for frying
4 cups bean sprouts, chopped cabbage or assorted fresh greens

Cut marlin into ¾-inch bite-size cubes; place in mixing bowl with soy sauce, onions, ogo and sesame oil; mix well.

In a hot wok, add oil and quickly sear the fish. Cook only for about a minute, keeping the centers of the marlin cubes raw. To serve, divide bean sprouts, chopped cabbage or greens into individual plates and top with fried marlin poke.

Note: For this recipe, no other fish works as well as marlin.

'Ahi Poke Musubi

The Kahala Hotel & Resort

Yield: 4 musubi

This is an expansion of The Kahala Hotel & Resort's recipe. Here's a way to take basic picnic food uptown. This popular appetizer at one of Honolulu's swankiest restaurants has its beginnings in a plain ball of rice that can't be more ordinary. But stuffed with poke, rolled in furikake and fried, it becomes worthy of fine dining.

> 2 cups cooked short-grain rice (hot/steamed)
> ½ (2.65 oz.) package of sushinoko (powdered sushi vinegar mix; see note)
> 1 cup 'Ahi Shoyu Poke (see opposite page)
> ½ cup furikake
> 2 cups vegetable oil for frying
> Baby Romaine lettuce leaves
> Crab Namasu (see page 48)

Combine hot rice and sushinoko to make sushi rice.

Spread ¼ cup sushi rice on a piece of plastic wrap so that it is about ½-inch thick. Place ¼ cup 'Ahi Shoyu Poke in center of rice and cover with ¼ cup sushi rice. Form a ball using plastic wrap and bind rice to create a well-packed rice ball (musubi). Remove plastic wrap and coat musubi with furikake. Repeat this process to continue making musubis.

Deep fry musubis in 350 to 375°F hot oil. Let musubis rest a minute to allow rice to become crunchy. Cut each musubi into 3 to 4 pieces and lightly coat poke center with soy sauce.

To plate each musubi serving, place 3 baby Romaine lettuce leaves equally spaced apart in a circle. Place namasu in center of leaves and arrange musubi pieces in between leaves.

Note: Sushinoko is available in the Oriental food aisle or at Asian grocery stores. If you would prefer to make your own sushi rice from scratch, follow the recipe on page 48.

'Ahi Shoyu Poke

Yield: About 1 cup

1 cup fresh 'ahi, finely diced
8 teaspoons minced green onion
2 Maui onions, finely diced
½ cup soy sauce
½ teaspoon grated fresh ginger
1 teaspoon sesame seeds
Sesame oil to taste

Combine all ingredients; toss to mix well.

(continued on the next page)

Crab Namasu

Yield: About 2 cups

Salt
2 oz. Japanese cucumber, cut into ¼-inch slices
1 oz. daikon, cut into ¼-inch slices
½ oz. minced green onion
1 oz. crab meat lumps
2 tablespoons Vinegar Sauce (see below)

Vinegar Sauce:

1¾ cups rice vinegar
¾ cup sugar
1 tablespoon finely minced fresh ginger
Salt to taste

Salt cucumber and daikon; let stand 30 to 60 minutes; rinse, drain, and squeeze out excess water. Combine with green onion and crab. Mix together ingredients for Vinegar Sauce and pour over vegetables; toss to mix well. Chill before serving.

Sushi Rice

Yield: 9 cups cooked

3 cups rice
3 cups water

Vinegar Sauce:

½ cup rice vinegar
½ cup sugar
1 teaspoon salt
2 tablespoons mirin (sweet rice wine, optional)

Wash rice and drain. Add water, cover and bring to a boil; reduce heat to simmer and cook 5 to 8 minutes or until water level reduced to level of rice. Cook additional 7 to 8 minutes over low heat. Turn heat off and allow rice to steam, covered, for 10 minutes before transferring to large bowl.

Combine Vinegar Sauce ingredients; heat until sugar dissolves; cool. Gradually pour half over hot rice and toss gently. Add more Vinegar Sauce, if desired. Fan to cool quickly. Rice is now ready to make various types of sushi.

Hawaiian Pulehu Tri-tip Steak

Yield: 4 to 6 servings

Pulehu is a Hawaiian technique—literally "to broil." These strips of beef are grilled over hot coals, turned frequently to produce an even, smoky finish. It really couldn't be simpler—no marinades to slosh around, no fancy ingredients—making this a perfect way to barbecue at the beach or a tailgate party. —MURIEL MIURA

2½ pounds tri-tip steak (triangular tip of the sirloin)
½ cup sea salt
1 tablespoon garlic, minced
½ tablespoon cracked peppercorns
1 tablespoon sugar

Prepare a charcoal grill. Rub salt, garlic, pepper and sugar into the meat and let sit 30 minutes. Place meat on grill and cook, turning the meat every 4 minutes. Total cooking time is about 10 to 15 minutes, depending upon the thickness of the cut.

Baked Stuffed Shrimp

Jameson's by the Sea

Yield: 8 servings

Jameson's By the Sea overlooks Magic Sands Beach on the Kona Coast. Great view, great food—a fine place for a celebration. One of my favorite dishes here is the shrimp stuffed with crabmeat and white fish. —AUDREY WILSON

48 large shrimp, butterflied

Cheese Sauce:

1½ cups milk
3 cups grated or shredded sharp cheese
¼ cup butter
¼ cup flour
Dash of salt
Dash of dry mustard
Dash of white pepper
Dash of Worcestershire sauce
(Here, a dash is approximately ¹⁄₁₆ of a teaspoon)

Stuffing:

¾ cup minced onions
¼ cup minced celery
2 tablespoons minced parsley
¼ cup butter
1 tablespoon sherry
¼ pound Dungeness crab meat
¼ pound white fish, steamed
½ pound bread crumbs

Hollandaise sauce:

24 ounces butter (6 sticks)
5 egg yolks, beaten
⅛ teaspoon cayenne pepper
1 tablespoon lemon juice

To prepare the cheese sauce: Heat the butter in a saucepot over medium heat. Mix the flour into the melted butter and whisk until you have a smooth paste (the roux). Add the dry mustard, salt, and pepper to the roux and mix well. Slowly add the milk to the roux, mixing with a whisk the whole time to prevent lumps. As the milk and roux heat, the mixture will thicken. Add the Worcestershire sauce and shredded sharp cheddar cheese. Cook briefly until the cheese melts and remove from heat.

To prepare the stuffing: Sauté the minced onions and celery in the butter until tender, then add the parsley and sherry; mix well. In a large mixing bowl, combine the crabmeat, fish, and the cheese sauce. Then tip the onion and celery mixture into the bowl and mix well. Divide the stuffing into 24 equal portions. Form each dab of stuffing into a shrimp-sized wedge.

To prepare the Hollandaise sauce: Heat the butter in a heavy saucepan or the top of a double boiler until it is hot and foamy, but not browned.

In a small bowl, whisk or beat egg yolks with the lemon juice and cayenne pepper. Gradually add the butter to the egg yolks, whisking as you pour. Don't add the butter all at once or the eggs will curdle. Return the sauce to the saucepan or double boiler and beat over low heat until the sauce thickens slightly.

To prepare the shrimp: Stack shrimp in pairs. Place wedges of stuffing on top of shrimp and place on baking sheet. Bake at 350°F for 5 minutes or until shrimp are cooked.

Serve the stuffed shrimp with the Hollandaise sauce.

Tangled Tiger Prawns with Pineapple-Chili-Garlic Sauce

Yield: 4 servings

Maui's annual Taste of Lahaina festival features restaurant booths serving toothsome samples, live music, and rides for the keiki and young at heart. Restaurants showcase their tastiest recipes here and hope to win. This recipe, we're proud to say, debuted at the festival and won both the best seafood and best of show categories. The sauce compliments this dish as the vinegar will cut the oil. —Tylun Pang

12 each (21/15) tiger prawns, peeled and deveined
4 ounce katafi (shredded phyllo dough)
1 teaspoon sake
1 teaspoon lime juice
½ teaspoon salt
Oil for deep-frying

Pineapple-Chili-Garlic Sauce:

½ cup pineapple, diced (¼-inch)
1 tablespoon minced Maui onion
2 cloves garlic, finely chopped
1 tablespoon chopped cilantro
½ cup sugar
½ cup rice wine vinegar
1 teaspoon sambal oelek (Indonesian chili paste)

To make the sauce, cut up the pineapple, onion, garlic, and cilantro per the instructions in the ingredients list. Put the pineapple, onion, garlic, sugar, vinegar, and sambal oelek in a saucepan over medium-high heat and bring to a boil for 2 minutes. Remove from the heat and let cool. Stir in the chopped cilantro just before serving.

Marinate the prawns with the sake, lime juice, and salt for 20 minutes.

Thread the marinated prawns from the tail end onto each of the (6-inch) bamboo skewers. Divide the shredded phyllo into 12 even strands and lay the skewered prawns at one end of the phyllo strands and wrap around the prawns, tangling them up.

Heat oil in your deep-fryer or a deep pot to 350°F. Deep-fry the skewered prawns for 1½ to 2 minutes, or until they are golden brown. You will probably have to do this in several batches; don't crowd the oil. Drain the prawns on paper towels.

Divide the chili-garlic sauce into small bowls and serve alongside these crispy prawn skewers.

Pipikaula

(Beef Jerky)

Yield: 6 to 8 servings

At Helena's Hawaiian Foods in Kalihi, the pipikaula hangs in strips over the grill, absorbing flavor all day long as it slowly dries. This is a technique you probably can't reproduce at home, but it illustrates the personal touch that can go into this dried-meat dish. Some people use smokers to cure the meat, but in this case its done in the oven at low heat, to create a local form of beef jerky.

4 pound flank steak, cut into 2-inch wide strips

Marinade:

1 cup soy sauce
½ cup sake (rice wine) or dry sherry
2 cloves garlic, finely minced
1 small piece fresh ginger, minced
2 Hawaiian red chili peppers, seeded and minced
2 tablespoons sugar
1 teaspoon Hawaiian (rock) salt
1 tablespoon liquid smoke
½ teaspoon white pepper

Combine all marinade ingredients in zip-top plastic bag; mix well. Marinate beef in marinade overnight, turning several times. Drain meat and arrange on cooling racks set on foil-lined baking sheets. Dry meat in oven set at 200°F for 7 to 8 hours or until of "jerky" texture. Meat may be stored in refrigerator up to 5 days or in the freezer 6 to 8 months. Slice diagonally to serve. If desired, meat slices may be heated in hot oil in skillet before serving.

Tip: Soak garlic cloves in cold water for 15 minutes, then drain and refrigerate, uncovered, overnight to making peeling easier.

Lumpia

(Filipino Fried Spring Rolls)

Yield: About 40 rolls

This fried finger food is the Filipino equivalent of Chinese egg rolls or Southeast Asian spring rolls. Fillings run the gamut, but typically include ground meat and bean sprouts, although vegetarian versions abound, and a banana-filled lumpia is a popular dessert. Key to the dish is the dipping sauce, a sweet-sour mixture of vinegar, sugar and ketchup that ties all the flavors together. —Muriel Miura

½ pound lean ground pork or beef
½ pound ground chicken
½ pound shrimp, shelled and chopped
2 cloves garlic, crushed
1 medium onion, minced
1 package (12 oz.) bean sprouts, washed and drained
1 medium carrot, shredded
1 cup cabbage, shredded
½ cup raisins, optional
1½ teaspoons salt
¼ teaspoon white pepper
1 tablespoon patis (fish sauce)
2 tablespoons flour
2 to 3 tablespoons water
40 lumpia wrappers
Canola or vegetable oil for frying

Sweet-Sour Sauce:

⅓ cup water
⅓ cup vinegar
⅓ cup sugar
1 teaspoon cornstarch
1 teaspoon ketchup
Salt and pepper to taste

Brown meat, chicken, and shrimp with garlic and onion in large saucepan. Add vegetables, raisins, and seasonings; cook for 2 minutes over high heat. Drain and cool.

Combine flour and water to make paste. To make lumpia, place 2 tablespoons of filling on a lumpia wrapper. Fold nearest edge of wrapper over filling; fold left and right sides toward center and roll lightly toward open edge. Seal with flour paste. Fry until golden brown in oil heated to 375°F. Drain on absorbent paper and serve with Sweet-Sour Sauce.

To prepare Sweet-Sour Sauce, mix all ingredients together in a small saucepan; cook over low heat until thickened.

Fried Veggie Fishcake

Guy Watanabe

Yield: About 20 pieces

Chinese fishcake is one of the least appealing items you'll find at the seafood counter. Gray and shiny, it looks like a soft, pale version of beef liver—totally unappetizing. But flavored and fried, it's quite delicious, and an economical way to bring fish to the table. Even those who don't like commercial Japanese kamaboko can appreciate the freshness of a homemade fishcake patty.

1 pound raw Chinese fishcake
3 teaspoons cornstarch
2 teaspoons sugar
2 teaspoons mayonnaise
1 egg, slightly beaten
⅓ cup chopped green beans (instead of string beans)
⅓ cup chopped carrots
⅓ cup chopped water chestnuts
2 cups oil for deep frying

Mix all ingredients together in a large mixing bowl. Drop by tablespoonfuls into oil heated to 375°F until puffy and golden brown on all sides. Drain on absorbent paper and serve hot or at room temperature as pūpū or side dish.

~ **Variations: Char Siu Fishcake:** *Add ⅓ cup diced char siu to above mixture.* **Shrimp Fishcake:** *Add ⅓ cup diced fresh shrimp to above mixture.*

~ **Note:** *Use rice oil for cleaner tasting fishcakes.*

~ **Of interest:** *Chinese fishcake is made in Hawai'i, usually from 'ō'io or awa'aua—bonefish or ladyfish, respectively. The soft flesh is scraped from the bones, then mashed and strained to produce a smooth, jelly-like product. A little water and salt are added. It can be fried as is, or combined with cornstarch, egg and basic flavorings such as green onions and oyster sauce. Find it at fishmarkets or Asian groceries.*

One of Hawai'i's treats is to stop at a lunch wagon or local drive-in for a plate lunch. It's like being in culinary heaven to walk up to the window and smell all the different main dishes cooking—teriyaki, kal bi, laulau, local-style chicken long rice to name just a few. All these ethnic foods have become plate lunch staples, accompanied with the ever constant side order of macaroni or potato salad.

When people are asked for their favorite foods, by far the greatest number say plate lunch, with their protein element—teriyaki chicken, beef curry, Hawaiian stew, garlic chicken, etc.—along with two scoops of rice and macaroni salad.

While there are now chain restaurants serving "local grinds," the heart of this aspect of our culinary culture remains in small family operations dedicated to the perpetuation of the plate lunch. Plate-lunch food is our comfort food—what we crave for when away from Hawai'i. It's the food that says "home."

PLATE LUNCH FAVORITES

Chicken Katsu

L&L Drive-Inn

Yield: 10 servings

Who needs KFC when you've got Chicken Katsu? Katsu is a Japanese cutlet, most commonly made with pork and called tonkatsu. It's breaded and fried, then served in strips with a deep, dark sauce that draws its distinctive taste from Worcestershire sauce and ketchup. In Hawai'i, though, the chicken version is most popular, especially with kids. In fact, at L&L Drive-Inn, owner Eddie Flores says it's his top seller.

4 pounds (15 to 20) chicken thighs, boned, skinned and flattened
1 pound panko (Japanese style bread crumbs)

Batter:

2 eggs
¾ cup cornstarch
¼ teaspoon each salt, white pepper and garlic powder
1 cup water

Katsu Sauce:

¼ cup Worcestershire sauce
½ cup ketchup
½ cup sugar
1¼ cups water
¼ teaspoon salt
⅛ teaspoon each chicken bouillon, white pepper, and garlic powder
Dashes hot sauce (Tabasco brand preferred)

Combine Batter ingredients. Coat chicken in batter, then in panko. Fry in oil heated to 325°F until brown and crispy; cut into strips and serve with Katsu Sauce.

To make Sauce, combine all ingredients and bring to a boil. To thicken, add a small amount of cornstarch dissolved in water. Chill.

Variation: **Tonkatsu (Pork Cutlet):** *Substitute lean pork slices for chicken.*

Masu's Teriyaki Chicken

Masu's Massive Plate Lunch (Honolulu)

Yield: 10 servings

This recipe comes from the king of the plate lunch, Paul Masuoka of Masu's Massive Plate Lunch. It is broken down from a massive (of course) original that started with 3 gallons of soy sauce. These reduced proportions will give you enough sauce to coat the chicken, but at Masu's the chicken was submerged in sauce. To accomplish that, you should double the amount of sauce, pour it over the chicken and keep it warm for a couple of hours before serving.

1 tablespoon vegetable oil
5 pounds chicken thighs, bone-in, with skin
2 tablespoons cornstarch, dissolved in 1 tablespoon water

Sauce:

½ cup sugar
1 cup water
¾ cup soy sauce (Aloha brand preferred)
½ inch piece ginger, smashed
1 clove garlic, smashed

Preheat oven to 350°F. Combine sauce ingredients in pot and bring to boil. Turn off heat and stir to dissolve sugar. Remove ½ cup of sauce for dipping; set aside remainder.

Heat oil in heavy skillet, preferably cast-iron, over high heat. Dip chicken pieces in the ½ cup sauce, then sear in skillet, working in batches. (Masuoka says this step should be very smoky, so the chicken takes on a smoky taste. If you have a portable gas grill, the searing is best done outside.) Place seared pieces in baking pan, skin side down. Pour any remaining dipping sauce over chicken. Bake in 350°F oven for 60 to 70 minutes or until cooked through. Remove garlic and ginger from reserved sauce. Bring sauce to simmer. Stir in cornstarch slurry and stir to thicken. Pour sauce over chicken.

Teriyaki Sauce

Masu's Massive Plate Lunch (Honolulu)

Yield: About 9 cups

Here we have the basic Japanese formula: soy sauce, sugar, ginger, garlic. In various proportions and with various additions you'll find this mixture in teriyaki, hekka, sukiyaki, niitsuke...and on and on. If you're making teriyaki for a crowd, here's a more massive version. The sauce can be used with beef, pork, or fish as well.

3 cups soy sauce
4 cups water
2 cups sugar
Fresh ginger to taste, smashed
Garlic to taste, smashed

Combine all ingredients in saucepan; bring to a boil over medium heat. Stir to dissolve sugar and store in covered jar in refrigerator until ready to use as marinade, dipping, basting, or cooking sauce for a variety of meats and dishes.

Variations:

Teriyaki Beef: Marinate thin slices of beef in Teriyaki Sauce 30 to 60 minutes before broiling or pan-frying.

Teriyaki Fish: Cook whole fish or fish fillets in Teriyaki Sauce. Fish may also be broiled using Teriyaki Sauce for basting or pan-fried with sauce poured over to serve.

Teriyaki Pork: Marinate thin slices of lean pork in Teriyaki Sauce 30 to 60 minutes before broiling or pan-frying.

Note: For those who insist on having sake or mirin in their teriyaki sauce, add about 1 cup mirin or sake.

Sweet and Sour Spareribs

Yield: 6 servings

The Chinese came early to the Islands. A few Chinese sailors accompanied Captain Cook in 1778, and the first Chinese indentured laborers were imported in 1852. These immigrants were single men who often married Hawaiian women. Others brought wives from China. They left the plantations, started stores and farms of their own, and prospered. Chinese food, bought from the itinerant manapua man or consumed at an inexpensive Chinese restaurant, became popular with all ethnic groups.

1 pound spareribs
1½ tablespoons soy sauce
1 tablespoon + ½ cup brown sugar
1½ tablespoons cornstarch
1 tablespoon canola oil
4 cloves garlic, chopped coarsely
4 (½-inch) slices of ginger
⅓ cup white vinegar
½ cup water

Sweet and sour spareribs is a favorite Chinese dish. These spareribs are marinated overnight so that the meat is infused with the sweet tang of soy sauce and sugar.

I like my ribs with daikon and carrot pickle. The tart vegetables complement the sweet meat.

Make the marinade by mixing the soy sauce, 1 tablespoon of the brown sugar, and the cornstarch. Put the spareribs into a 1-gallon size re-sealable plastic bag and pour the marinade over the ribs. Seal the bag and leave it in the refrigerator overnight. Turn the bag a couple of times to make sure that all the meat is evenly marinated.

The next day, heat the canola oil in a medium sized stew pot over a brisk heat. When it's hot, add the marinated ribs. Keep turning them so that they brown on all sides. The cornstarch from the marinade may stick to the bottom of the pan; don't worry about it, just scrape it up with a spatula before it hardens. The cornstarch will thicken the sauce later. When the ribs are brown, add the garlic and ginger and sauté for a few more minutes.

Add the vinegar, water, and the rest of the brown sugar. Cook on low heat for 1½ hours, until the spareribs are soft and the sauce is thick.

Tonkatsu

(Pork Cutlet)

Yield: 4 servings

y way! My version of tonkatsu sauce. This sauce can also be used with chicken. —TYLUN PANG

4 slices (4 ounces each) boneless pork loin
½ teaspoon salt
¼ teaspoon pepper
½ cup flour
2 eggs, beaten
1 cup panko (Japanese-style bread crumbs)
4 tablespoons vegetable oil for frying
1 cup shredded napa cabbage

Tonkatsu Sauce (makes ½ cup):

2 tablespoons peeled and grated ginger
½ cup ketchup
¼ cup sugar
2 tablespoons Worcestershire sauce
½ teaspoon Coleman's mustard powder

To prepare the sauce, peel and grate the ginger. Combine all ingredients in a small saucepan and bring to a boil over medium-high heat. Simmer for 2 minutes. Cool before serving.

Season the pork slices with the salt and pepper. Dredge the pork slices in flour and dip in the beaten egg. Let excess egg drip off. Put the slices in a pan of panko and coat evenly.

Heat vegetable oil in a frying pan over medium high heat. Fry the pork cutlets on both sides until they are crisp and golden brown. Drain on a paper towel. Before serving, slice the cutlets into strips and arrange on shredded napa cabbage. Serve with Tonkatsu Sauce.

Kalbi

(Korean-Style Barbecued Shortribs)

Yield: 4 to 6 servings

These grilled shortribs are the Korean answer to Japanese teriyaki, and probably the dish by which Korean barbecue restaurants in Hawai'i are judged. Compared to teriyaki, the marinade is similar in its mixture of salty and sweet—soy sauce and sugar—but leans more toward garlic where teriyaki leans to ginger. Sesame oil and sesame seeds complete the package. —Muriel Miura

3 pounds English cut (thick) shortribs, scored

Marinade:

½ cup soy sauce
¼ cup sesame oil
¼ cup sugar
2 cloves garlic, minced
¼ teaspoon salt
¼ teaspoon black pepper
3 stalks green onions, minced
2 teaspoons toasted sesame seeds

Combine Marinade ingredients and pour over shortribs in zip-top plastic bag; marinate overnight in refrigerator. Broil 8 to 10 minutes on each side until of desired doneness.

Variations:

Barbecued Chicken: *Substitute chicken for beef shortribs.*

Kun Koki (Korean-Style Barbecued Beef): *Substitute flank steak (tendon removed and meat trimmed).*

Meatloaf

Yield: 6 to 8 servings

What's Hawaiian about meatloaf? Nothing, but we do have our own way of eating it: with LOTS of brown gravy, rather than the tomato-based or barbecue sauces used in the rest of the country. It's a favorite on the menus of family restaurants and plate-lunch spots—a once-a-week special, at least. At home, meatloaf is fast and easy to prepare, inexpensive and versatile. For a true local touch, try pouring teriyaki sauce over your meatloaf during the last 15 minutes of baking. Leftovers in sandwiches are also 'ono. —MURIEL MIURA

1 pound lean ground beef
½ pound lean ground pork
1½ teaspoons salt
1/8 teaspoon black pepper
1 egg, beaten
½ cup chopped onion
¼ cup milk
½ cup bread crumbs
¼ cup tomato ketchup

Brown gravy (see page 2)

Combine all ingredients; mix thoroughly. Place in 9 x 5-inch loaf pan. Bake at 350°F for 40 to 50 minutes or until done. Serve with brown gravy or ketchup.

Hawaiian Beef Curry Stew

Yield: 12 servings

This full-bodied curry stew is so good, it will attract a crowd. Bits of beef are slow-cooked until juicy and tender, and crisp vegetables are added to give the dish some texture, taste, and color. —MURIEL MIURA

2½ pounds chuck or stew
   meat
¾ cup flour
2 tablespoons canola oil
1 clove garlic, minced
2 medium onions, wedged
2 teaspoons salt
¼ teaspoon pepper
2 ½ quarts water

2 ribs celery, sliced diagonally
4 carrots, pared and cut into
   1-inch pieces
4 potatoes, pared and cut into
   1-inch pieces
2 tablespoons curry powder
   or more, if desired
½ cup flour
1 cup water

Dredge meat in flour; brown meat in hot oil. Add garlic, onion, salt and pepper; stir. Add 2½ quarts water; cover and simmer for 1½ to 2 hours or until meat is tender. Add celery, carrots and potatoes; cover and simmer 20 to 30 minutes. Mix curry powder and flour with water and slowly stir into stew; cook, stirring constantly, until mixture thickens. Adjust seasoning as necessary.

Potato-Macaroni Salad

Yield: 10 servings

A salad, by Webster's definition, is a cold dish of vegetables or fruits "in various combinations, served with a dressing, or molded in gelatin, and sometimes with seafood, poultry, eggs, etc., added..." This does nothing to explain macaroni salad, which is 95 percent pasta and 4.8 percent mayonnaise. The only part of the definition that it meets is "cold." And maybe "etc." At any rate, Hawai'i's version is distinctive by the amount of mayo used. Many experts have pondered how it came to be so ubiquitous, and they can only speculate. The best guess is that islanders became exposed to the mainland potato salad tradition and found macaroni to be a cheaper approach. Simple as that.

¾ pound Gem salad potato
1 pound elbow macaroni
¼ cup finely diced carrot
3 tablespoons finely diced celery
3 tablespoons finely diced onion
1 large hard boiled egg, grated
1½ pounds mayonnaise
Salt and pepper to taste

Cover potatoes with tap water; boil until cooked on the firm side. Cool in water; peel and cut into ¼-inch cubes. Boil macaroni until cooked on the firm side; rinse in a colander with water. Thoroughly mix potato, macaroni, carrot, celery, onion, egg and a little salt and pepper. Add mayonnaise and mix well to desired consistency. Salt and pepper to taste.

Tip: Add a little white vinegar when boiling potatoes; the acidity helps the potatoes cook evenly and prevents them from falling apart.

"Finger-lickin' good" chicken recipes featuring some of the fusion flavors of Hawai'i are highlighted here. Chicken is the protein of choice for many island cooks because of its versatility with countless other ingredients and flavors. In addition, it can be cooked in many ways: fried, broiled, poached, boiled, roasted and grilled. It's no surprise that tapping the ethnic flavors of Hawai'i would make something as basic as chicken taste so good!

Leftover chicken can also be used to make delicious stir-fries, curries, salads and more. Dark meat can take a bit more cooking when reheating because it has more fat to prevent it from becoming dry and tough while white meat should be treated gently to retain its moisture.

MAIN DISHES
CHICKEN

Chicken or Squid Lū'au

Yield: 4 to 6 servings

The ancient Hawaiians revered taro, considered the elder brother of man and an intrinsic part of life. The leaf carries its own name, lū'au, from which the feast called the lū'au is derived. Dark green and deeply flavorful, the leaf is often used as a wrapper for meat or fish, but in this dish it becomes part of a soupy, comforting stew. Lū'au requires a long cooking time to break down the calcium oxalate crystals that can make the mouth burn and itch. On the mainland and other taro-deprived parts of the world, spinach and chard are often suggested as substitutes for lū'au. But they really aren't the same. Lucky you live Hawai'i. —MURIEL MIURA

2 pounds lū'au (taro leaves)
2¼ cups water
2 cups coconut milk
1 teaspoon salt
Cooked chicken or squid, cut
   into small pieces

Wash lū'au leaves; remove stems and fibrous part of veins. Place leaves in large saucepan; add water and bring to a boil; lower heat and simmer for 1 hour, stirring frequently; drain well. Stir in coconut milk, salt and chicken or squid; heat through but do not boil.

To prepare chicken: Cut 1¾ pounds boneless chicken thighs into small pieces. Sauté chicken in 2 tablespoons butter or margarine; cover and simmer 15 to 20 minutes.

To prepare squid: Cut 1½ pounds cooked squid or octopus into thin crosswise slices.

*~ **Tip:** Spinach leaves may be substituted for lū'au leaves.*

Chicken Long Rice

Yield: 6 to 8 servings

Soft, mild and approachable, chicken long rice is the easy-to-eat dish for timid diners who are overwhelmed by their first lū'au experience. Compared to the bold flavors of laulau or poke, this dish of chicken pieces and silky long rice noodles is comparatively bland—in color and in taste—making it a light counterpart to everything else on the table.

2¼ pounds chicken thighs
3 quarts water
1 tablespoon salt
1 tablespoon minced fresh
   ginger
1 large round onion, finely
   chopped
5 chicken bouillon cubes
8 ounces long rice
½ cup chopped green
   onions

Put chicken into large saucepan. Add 2 quarts of the water, salt and ginger; bring to a boil. Lower heat and skim; simmer for 40 to 50 minutes. Remove from heat and drain, saving broth. Remove meat from chicken, discarding bones. Cut meat into bite-size pieces; set aside. Put broth, onion, bouillon cubes and the remaining 1 quart water into saucepan; bring to a boil. Add long rice then lower heat and cook, covered, for 5 to 10 minutes. Turn off heat and let stand 20 to 30 minutes.

Cut long rice into 3 to 4 inch lengths with kitchen shears. Stir in chicken and heat briefly, if desired, before serving. Sprinkle with green onions before serving.

Roasted Lemon Soy Chicken

Yield: 4 to 6 servings

This recipe from one of my dearest friends, this dish puts a new spin on the traditional roasted chicken by infusing it with the zesty, clean flavors of ginger and lemon. —MURIEL MIURA

1 whole chicken (3 to 4 pounds), cleaned and dried

Marinade:

½ cup canola oil
⅓ cup fresh lemon juice
¼ cup soy sauce
1 clove garlic, minced
¾ teaspoon grated fresh ginger
½ teaspoon salt
¼ teaspoon pepper

Mix together all Marinade ingredients in bowl; Coat chicken with marinade. Cover and refrigerate 4 hours or overnight. Drain and place chicken on rack in foil lined roasting pan. Bake at 325°F for 1 hour or until meat thermometer inserted in thigh registers 170°F, brushing chicken occasionally while roasting. After removing from oven, let rest 20 minutes before serving.

> *Tip: If desired, reserve pan juices in roasting pan. Add ½ cup chicken broth, 2 tablespoons lemon juice and 1 teaspoon soy sauce; whisk, stirring to loosen brown bits, simmer until slightly thickened. Adjust seasoning as necessary. Serve with chicken.*

Korean-Style Spicy Chicken

Yield: 4 to 6 servings

This recipe for Korean-style spicy chicken is in the top five favorites at Kō, The Fairmont Kea Lani's signature restaurant on Maui. The chicken is marinated, served crisped with special sauce and drizzled with Ali'i Kula Lavender Farm Honey. —TYLUN PANG

1 pound boneless, skinless chicken thighs
1 cup cornstarch, for dredging
Oil, for deep-frying

Marinade:

2 teaspoons sugar
1 tablespoon soy sauce
2 teaspoons sake
1 teaspoon sesame oil
1 teaspoon salt

Dipping Sauce:

1 teaspoon minced garlic
½ teaspoon peeled and grated ginger
4 tablespoons brown sugar
4 tablespoons soy sauce
2 tablespoons mirin
1 teaspoon sesame oil
¼ teaspoon dried chili flakes
2 tablespoons water

Garnish:

Lavender honey (or honey of your choice)
Toasted sesame seeds
Finely chopped green onion

Mix marinade ingredients in a bowl. Cut the boneless chicken into 1½-inch chunks and place in the marinade. Marinate in refrigerator for at least 30 minutes.

Measure the cornstarch into a bowl or shallow-sided pan. Cover a baking sheet with plastic wrap. Drain the chicken chunks and dredge each piece in the cornstarch; lay the cornstarch-coated chicken pieces on the baking sheet and refrigerate for 20 minutes.

While the chicken is chilling, mix the dipping sauce. Peel and mince the garlic; peel and grate the ginger. Mix all sauce ingredients in a small bowl and set aside.

When the chicken has finished chilling, heat the oil in your deep-fryer or saucepot to 350°F (a frying thermometer will help you keep the oil at the proper temperature). Slip the chicken chunks into the hot oil and fry for 3 to 4 minutes, or until brown and crisp. Turn as necessary. You will probably need to do this in several batches; do not overcrowd the oil. Drain the fried chicken on paper towels to remove excess oil.

Presentation:

I like to dip all the chicken pieces in the sauce and drizzle them with honey. Sprinkles of toasted sesame seeds and finely sliced green onion complete the dish.

However, it's up to you if you'd like to just put out the dipping sauce and the garnishes next to a platter of fried chicken and let your family or guests season their own chicken.

Oven Fried Chicken

Yield: 10 to 12 servings

Fried Chicken is a quintessential American dish. It's widely beloved and featured on dining tables across the land. What's not so beloved, however, is the oil and grease the chicken is fried in (especially in these times of calorie counting consciousness). Here is an "oven fried" recipe that cuts out the grease and is just as delicious!

> 1½ cups buttermilk
> 1 teaspoon salt
> ½ teaspoon freshly ground black pepper
> 5 pounds chicken thighs, rinsed and dried
> 2 to 3 cups mayonnaise
> 1½ cups bread crumbs
> ½ cup flour
> 2 teaspoons salt
> 2 teaspoons paprika
> ¼ teaspoon pepper
> ¼ cup macadamia nut bits, optional

Mix together buttermilk, salt and ½ teaspoon pepper in large bowl; marinate chicken pieces overnight in refrigerator. In another bowl, mix together bread crumbs, flour, salt, paprika, pepper and macadamia nuts, if used; set aside. Remove chicken from buttermilk marinade and allow to "dry" in refrigerator for about 1 hour. Roll chicken pieces in mayonnaise then dredge in bread crumb mixture being careful to coat all sides of chicken. Place chicken, skin side down, on shallow oil sprayed foil-lined baking pan.

Bake at 350°F for 30 minutes. Turn and bake 30 additional minutes or until tender and done.

Cold Ginger Chicken

James H. Q. Lee (Owner), Hee Hing Restaurant

Yield: About 4 servings

This classic Chinese dish takes time to make and a lot of chopping, but the technique is simple: You poach a whole chicken in plain water, then chill and cut into pieces. It's the sauce that carries the flavor. Here some skill and patience at the chopping block is necessary as you'll need to very finely mince a large quantity of ginger and green onions. After that, just add oil and pour it on!

1 whole chicken (2½ to 3 lbs), wash and drain
6 quarts water
Ice water

Ginger Sauce:

¼ pound fresh ginger, washed, peeled and finely minced
½ pound green onions, washed and finely minced
8 ounces vegetable or soybean oil
1 tablespoon sesame seed oil
1 teaspoon salt
½ teaspoon white pepper

Chinese parsley
Chinese mustard paste
Soy sauce

Bring water to boil in large pot to hold water and chicken; immerse chicken in hot water to cover and reduce heat to lowest setting without turning off heat. Cover and let stand 45 to 60 minutes or until chicken is of desired doneness. Remove chicken from hot water and immerse into ice water. Cool chicken to room temperature; remove from water and chill in refrigerator for at lest 3 hours or until ready to serve. When ready to serve, chop chicken into serving pieces and place on serving platter. Spoon cold Ginger Sauce generously over chicken and garnish with Chinese parsley. Mix mustard and soy sauce for dipping. Set aside extra cold Ginger Sauce for dipping.

Combine all ingredients of Ginger Sauce in mixing bowl; whisk together to mix well and let stand for at least 2 hours before serving.

Nori Chicken

Yield: Approximately 12 strips of chicken

This crunchy chicken treat makes a great pūpū (appetizer) or picnic dish. Many Big Island okazu-yas (Hawaiian-style delicatessens) sell nori chicken. If you love it from the okazu-ya, why not try it at home?
—AUDREY WILSON

> **4 sheets of nori (crisp seaweed)**
> **1 pound boneless, skinless chicken thighs**
> **1 cup cornstarch**
>
> Sauce:
>
> **½ cup soy sauce**
> **4 teaspoons sugar**
> **2 teaspoons sake**

Slice the chicken into 1 x 2-inch pieces. Mix up the sauce. Marinate the chicken in the sauce for a minimum of one hour.

Cut the sheets of nori in half, then into ½-inch strips.

Dredge the marinated chicken pieces in cornstarch, then wrap a strip of nori around the middle of each piece. Deep fry the nori-wrapped chicken in hot, 350°F oil. Drain on paper towels.

{ MAIN DISHES—CHICKEN }

Garlic Chicken

Yield: 6 to 8 servings

These little nuggets of sweet-salty fried chicken are a standard choice at Japanese okazuya, or take-out delis. Mitsu-ken on North School Street is particularly well-known for Garlic Chicken—but won't share the recipe. The interesting thing about the dish is that it doesn't taste all that garlicky. In this recipe, in fact, it's just a clove in an otherwise standard teriyaki base.

3 pounds chicken drummettes or wings
2 cups flour
2 tablespoons garlic salt
½ teaspoon white pepper
¼ teaspoon garlic powder
1 quart canola oil for frying

Ginger-Soy Sauce:

1 cup soy sauce
1 cup sugar
½ cup water
¼ teaspoon fresh grated ginger
1 small clove garlic, grated
¼ cup minced green onion
Shichimi togarashi (red pepper mix) to taste, optional

Rinse chicken and pat dry; set aside. Combine flour, garlic salt, pepper, and garlic powder in gallon-size plastic bag; shake to mix well. Place chicken in plastic bag; shake to coat with flour mixture. Refrigerate 30 to 45 minutes.

Deep fry in oil heated to 365 to 375°F until chicken is golden. Drain on absorbent paper and dip in Ginger-Soy Sauce to serve.

Prepare Ginger-Soy Sauce: Combine all ingredients for Ginger-Soy Sauce; mix until well blended. Serve with fried chicken.

Tip: Store fresh ginger in the freezer for easier grating—also keeps for a long while.

Orange Chicken

(Batter Fried Chicken with Orange Sauce)

Yield: 6 to 8 servings

This dish has roots in a traditional Chinese dish, Chen Pi Gi, that shows up in Hunan, Szechuan, and Cantonese cooking. The traditional version is made with dried orange rind, giving it a much more assertive, fresher taste. The chicken is normally chopped with the bones left in. To suit Western tastes, the dish has morphed in this country into something a bit sweeter—and boneless. Orange Chicken at Panda Express restaurants is something of a pop-culture phenom, fiercely popular in Hawai'i as it is all over the country. At 900 Panda restaurants in 36 states, those little glazed nuggets are the No. 1 seller, accounting for 38 percent of sales, even though diners typically have 19 other menu choices. Panda won't give up the recipe, but here's one that's similar, with more of an orange flavor.

3 pounds boneless chicken breast
1 tablespoon sherry
1 tablespoon soy sauce
½ teaspoon salt
2 eggs
¼ cup cornstarch
½ teaspoon baking powder
2 cups canola oil for frying

Orange Sauce:
¼ cup sugar
½ teaspoon salt
1 tablespoon cornstarch
1 cup chicken broth
1 tablespoon orange juice
1 small orange, thinly sliced
2 tablespoons canola oil

In a bowl combine chicken with sherry, soy sauce, and ½ teaspoon salt; let stand for 15 minutes. In a small bowl, beat eggs. Add cornstarch and baking powder to form smooth batter. Coat chicken with batter and fry in 2 cups hot oil until browned. Drain on absorbent paper; cut chicken into 1½ x 1-inch pieces; set aside.

To make the sauce, combine sugar, salt, cornstarch, chicken broth, and orange juice in a bowl; set aside. In a skillet, stir-fry orange slices in 2 tablespoons of hot oil for 30 seconds; slowly stir in cornstarch mixture. Cook, stirring constantly, until sauce is thick and clear. Pour over chicken to serve.

Variation: **Lemon Chicken:** *Substitute lemon for orange; prepare as directed.*

Sunday Dinner Chicken Adobo

Maria Gamponia (Wailuku)

Yield: 4 to 6 servings

Filipinos often raised chickens in their backyard, as the Gamponia family did. Sonny Gamponia describes what happened on Sunday in his house. "Sunday was always the day Mom would slaughter a chicken. When I went into the kitchen for breakfast, there would be a big pot of hot water, in which the chicken had been dunked to loosen the feathers. The smell of wet feathers permeated the room and the plucked chicken sat in a bowl with blood draining down the sink." The Sunday chicken was ready to cook.

> **1 chicken, cut in small pieces**
> **1 teaspoon salt OR 1 tablespoon soy sauce**
> **3 cloves garlic**
> **½ teaspoon black whole peppercorns**
> **2 bay leaves**
> **⅛ cup vinegar**
> **1 cup water, chicken broth, beer, or coconut milk**
> **Vegetable oil**

Place chicken in saucepan with oil. Add salt, garlic, peppercorns, bay leaf, vinegar, and water. Cook at a high heat, then turn the burner down, cover, add a few chunks of pork and pork fat for flavor, and simmer until chicken is tender and liquid is evaporated.

As dishes many evolve over time, Maria Gamponia's son, Demetrio Gamponia Jr., also known as Sonny, has modernized the recipe. He has eliminated the pork and pork fat and cooks with boneless chicken. Here is his revised recipe.

Place chicken in saucepan. Add bay leaf, vinegar, salt, garlic, and peppercorns and vinegar. Cook at high heat until the mixture simmers, then turn the heat down until the liquid reduces and the chicken is poached and tender. Separate the chicken and the liquid. Brown the chicken in a little bit of vegetable oil. Pour the cooking liquid over the chicken and add ½ cup to 1 cup of water to make a thin sauce. Heat through.

Sonny says that having the chicken in sauce tastes better and much like the adobo found in the Philippines. He said he ordered a chicken dish at Gerard's in Lahaina a decade ago, and it tasted just like chicken adobo but, of course, it was French.

Cornflake Chicken

Side Street Inn

Yield: 4 servings

Cornflake Chicken is a dish that everyone's mom used to make, although some moms used breadcrumbs or panko. Still, when this recipe, from Colin Nishida of Side Street Inn, was printed in the *Honolulu Star-Bulletin* in December of 2006, it became an immediate favorite with readers. Probably because it's so simple and makes such sense (mayonnaise to keep the chicken moist; cornflakes for crunch without deep-frying). Of course, Colin learned it from his mom.

8 chicken thighs (about 3 pounds), skin removed
½ teaspoon salt
Pepper, to taste
3 tablespoons grated Parmesan cheese
½ cup mayonnaise
4 cups cornflakes, crushed

Preheat oven to 375°F. Sprinkle chicken on both sides with salt, pepper and cheese. Coat with mayonnaise, then roll in cornflakes. Bake for 45 minutes, until juices run clear.

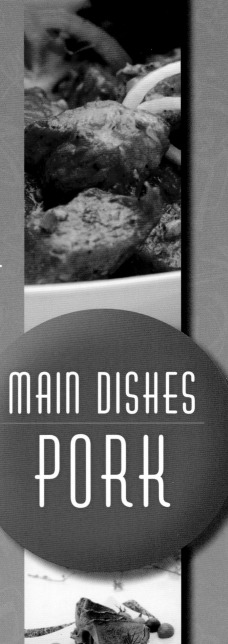

No cookbook of Hawai'i's favorite foods would be complete without kālua pork. Pork, considered to be "the other white meat," is a great protein source. Its mild taste allows it to be paired with any number of vegetables, spices and other ingredients. It also blends well with all glazes and sauces used by Island chefs and homemakers. As a result, pork is the meat of choice for many of Hawai'i's Asian cuisine. With a salty brine, a sweet glaze and the right cooking methods, you can have juicy, tasty pork every time.

MAIN DISHES
PORK

Baked Hoisin Barbecue Ribs

Yield: 6 to 8 servings

These pork ribs are flavored with hoisin—a spicy, salty-sweet brown sauce made of soybeans, sugar, garlic, Chinese five-spice powder, chili and red rice for coloring—and are then glazed with a layer of delicious honey. —MURIEL MIURA

2 racks of pork ribs
1 jar (15 oz.) hoisin sauce
1 jar (12 oz.) honey

Remove excess fat and tissues from ribs. Brush hoisin sauce on both sides and let stand in refrigerator overnight. Place pork ribs on rack on foil-lined baking pans. Brush with additional hoisin sauce on one side.

Bake at 350°F for 30 minutes; turn, brush with sauce on other side and bake additional 30 minutes or until done. Brush honey on both sides and leave in oven additional 5 minutes to glaze. Remove from oven, let stand 5 minutes before separating ribs. Cut into desired sizes to serve.

Adobo
(Filipino-Style Pickled Pork)
Chef Aurelio Garcia

Yield: 3 to 4 servings

Adobo is basic Filipino comfort food that can be found in hundreds of variations. It comes from a long tradition of meat dishes with a vinegar base, also found in the cuisines of Spain and France. Vinegar gives adobo its tang, but when correctly made, the dish should be a good balance of flavors.

- **2 pounds fresh pork butt, medium cubed**
- **1 teaspoon garlic salt**
- **½ teaspoon ground black pepper**
- **½ cup soy sauce**
- **1 tablespoon fresh minced garlic**
- **⅓ cup cider vinegar**
- **4 bay leaves, crumbled**

Combine all ingredients; mix well and marinate pork overnight in refrigerator. Place everything in a skillet; cover and cook over medium heat, stirring occasionally, until pork is browned and tender, about 30 to 45 minutes. Meat will be crispy on outside and all liquid in pan will have been absorbed. Serve very hot; may be reheated the next day.

*Variation: **Chicken Adobo:** Substitute 3 pounds chicken, cut into serving pieces, for pork; add 1 tablespoon grated ginger to sauce mixture.*

Roast Pork With Rosemary

Yield: About 12 servings

Pork is a versatile meat and can be served with anything, anytime of the week. Still, you'll want to change things up once in a while. This dish of rosemary infused pork roast adds wonderful flavor to an already tasty ingredient! —MURIEL MIURA

3 to 4 pound pork loin or Boston butt roast
2 tablespoons chopped fresh rosemary
4 cloves garlic, minced
1 teaspoon salt
½ teaspoon pepper
1 tablespoon margarine or butter
¼ cup chopped onion
2 tablespoons canola oil

Trim fat from pork roast. Mix rosemary and garlic. Make 8 to 10 deep slits about 2-inches apart in pork with sharp knife; insert small amounts of garlic mixture into slits. Sprinkle pork with salt and pepper.

Melt margarine or butter in shallow roasting pan in oven; sprinkle with onion. Place pork on rack in roasting pan; drizzle with canola oil. Insert meat thermometer so that tip is in center of thickest part of pork but does not touch fat. Roast, uncovered at 350°F for 1¾ to 2 hours or until thermometer reads 160°F. Let stand 15 minutes before slicing. Serve with gravy using your favorite recipe.

Oven Roasted Kālua Pork

Yield: Approximately 4 cups cooked pork

The imu, or earth oven, is the traditional Hawaiian way to make kālua pig. An imu is a large pit filled with rocks. Imu-makers build a fire on top of the rocks; when the fire dies down, the rocks remain extremely hot. The cooks put a cleaned, leaf-wrapped whole pig (plus leaf-wrapped bundles of other tasty foods) on top of the rocks, cover the pit with leaves, burlap sacks, and loose dirt, then let the food roast and steam overnight. Imu-cooked pig—real kālua pork—is moist, smoky, tender, and delicious.

Some Big Island folk still have imus in their back yards and cook pigs for special occasions, such as Christmas, weddings, and birthdays. The rest of us make kālua pork in our ovens. Here's a recipe used by many locals. —Audrey Wilson

> 6 pounds pork butt, scored at 2-inch intervals
> 2 tablespoons liquid smoke
> 3 tablespoons coarse salt
> (Hawaiian salt if possible; kosher salt will do)
> 14 ti leaves, stems removed
> Heavy aluminum foil

Wash the ti leaves and arrange them in a circle, as a whorl of overlapping leaves. Put the scored pork butt in a large roasting pan and rub it all over with salt and liquid smoke. Then take the meat out of the pan and put it, fat side up, on the ti leaves. Fold the ti leaves over the pork butt so that it is completely covered; tie the bundle securely with string. Place the wrapped butt on a sheet of heavy aluminum foil and wrap the foil tightly around the pork and ti leaves. The foil must be sealed, with tightly rolled seams, so that no steam can escape.

Place the package in a shallow roasting pan and roast in a 450°F oven for one hour. Reduce heat to 400°F and bake four hours longer.

Kālua pork is usually served shredded.

Delicious meals don't have to be difficult to make. Meet your new favorite beef entrée in Paniolo Rib Eye Steak. Turn this restaurant classic into your signature specialty— simply serve with a creamed spinach sauce for that gourmet touch.

These beef recipes reflect Hawai'i's ethnic cuisines and culinary traditions with colorful flavors, savory seasonings and unique cooking styles. Meals will become even more mouthwatering with range-raised naturally-fed island cattle. Hawai'i is fortunate that many local ranches, particularly the independents, are moving in this direction.

MAIN DISHES
BEEF

Paniolo Chili

Yield: 6 servings

Mexican cowboys (español, or paniolo in the Hawaiian language) were brought to the Big Island to teach Hawaiians how to herd and rope cattle. Native Hawaiians became superlative cowboys; one paniolo, Ikaika Purdy, won many mainland rodeo contests.

The original paniolos also brought Mexican and Western U.S. campfire cuisine to Hawai'i. Here's an easy chili recipe made with canned ingredients, just the kind of food that would be carried in a chuckwagon.

1 (12 oz.) Portuguese sausage, sliced into ¼-inch rounds
1 pound lean ground beef
2 cups chopped onion (approximately 1 large onion)
Oil for sautéing
2 cans (15 oz.) pork and beans, including sauce
1 can (14.5 oz.) stewed tomatoes, including juice
1 can (11 oz.) whole kernel corn, drained
1 can (6 oz.) olives, drained
1 can (4 oz.) mushrooms, either whole or stems and pieces, drained
1 can (8 oz.) tomato sauce
Salt to taste

Coat the bottom of a large pot with cooking oil and heat over medium-high heat. Add the ground beef and onions; sauté. Break up any large chunks of meat. When the hamburger is cooked, add the sliced Portuguese sausage. Continue cooking until the sausage is slightly browned and the onions are soft.

Drain off any excess fat. Add the remaining ingredients. Lower the heat until the chili is just simmering. Simmer the stew for 25 minutes. Add salt to taste before serving.

Granny's Hawaiian-Style Stew

Helen Leina'ala Watson Shaw, Wailuku

Yield: 8 servings

In the Hawaiian way, Robbie St. Sure Lum learned this recipe and the next by working with her granny, Helen Shaw, in the kitchen. Robbie was a boarder at Kamehameha Schools and, whenever she would come home to Maui on vacation, her granny would have a big pot of the following stew ready with poi, quartered Maui onion with Hawaiian salt, and chili pepper water. Depending on the time of year, they would also have līpoa cut up and sprinkled over the stew. The meal always ended with cold cut-up mango. Hawaiian comfort food!

- **2 pounds brisket meat, bone-in**
- **2 pounds boneless meat**
- **1 Maui onion, cut in wedges**
- **5 cloves garlic, gently smashed**
- **½ cup celery, including the leaf**
- **1 cup flour**
- **2 tablespoons Worcestershire sauce**
- **2 tablespoons soy sauce**
- **2 cups water**
- **1 can chicken broth**
- **1 small can tomato sauce**
- **4 beef bouillon cubes**
- **2 small bay leaves**
- **5 carrots, chunked**
- **2 stalks of celery, in large slices**
- **3 large potatoes, chunked**
- **4 tablespoons cornstarch mixed well with a little cold water**

In a large pot, sauté onions, garlic, and ½ cup celery with leaves. Remove. Add oil to pan and coat stew meat and brisket with flour and brown well. The more crispy and brown the meat is, the more 'ono the stew will be. Return sautéed vegetables to pot. Then add Worcestershire sauce, soy sauce, water, chicken broth, tomato sauce, bouillon, and bay leaves. Cook until meat is tender, about an hour. Add carrots, celery and potato and cook until done. Add cornstarch mixture to thicken. Add salt and pepper to taste.

Beef Juhn

(Batter-Fried Beef)

Yield: 6 servings

The juhn dishes—beef, fish, and sometimes even oyster—are the more delicate in the Korean repertoire, consisting of thin slices of meat dipped in an egg batter and pan-fried. That part's pretty basic. Where restaurants distinguish themselves is in the dipping sauce, which begins with ko choo jung—a Korean hot sauce made with soy bean paste, vinegar, chilies, and garlic.

1½ pounds sirloin or tri-tip steak
½ cup soy sauce
2 tablespoons minced green onion
1 tablespoon toasted sesame seeds
1 tablespoon sesame oil
1 tablespoon sugar
1 cup flour
4 eggs, beaten
1 cup canola oil

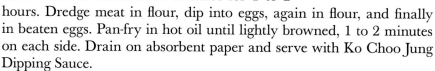

Slice meat ¼-inch thick, then cut into 4-inch squares; set aside. Combine soy sauce, green onion, sesame seeds, sesame oil, and sugar; mix well. Marinate meat slices in sauce for 1 to 2 hours. Dredge meat in flour, dip into eggs, again in flour, and finally in beaten eggs. Pan-fry in hot oil until lightly browned, 1 to 2 minutes on each side. Drain on absorbent paper and serve with Ko Choo Jung Dipping Sauce.

Ko Choo Jung Dipping Sauce (Korean Hot Dip)

Yield: 1½ cups

½ cup soy sauce
3 tablespoons toasted sesame seeds
3 tablespoons ko choo jung sauce
½ cup vinegar
½ cup sugar

Combine all ingredients in a jar; cover and shake vigorously. Serve with meat and vegetable dishes.

Teriyaki Beef Rib-Eye

Yield: 4 servings

Cupies Drive-In in Kahului is a favorite spot for great Maui grindz. Their breaded teriyaki beef is one of their most popular items. Now you can make it at home—and it's quick and easy too! For the full Cupies experience, enjoy your teri beef with freshly-cooked white rice and some mac salad. They make it for take out. —TYLUN PANG

> **2 pounds rib-eye steak, cut into ¼-inch slices**
> **½ cup flour for dredging meat**
> **4 tablespoons vegetable oil for sautéing**

Marinade:

> **1 teaspoon peeled and grated ginger**
> **2 medium cloves garlic, minced**
> **¾ cup soy sauce**
> **½ cup water**
> **¼ cup sugar**

Peel and grate the ginger; mince the garlic. Combine all the marinade ingredients in a bowl and mix well. Add the sliced rib-eye steak. Marinate the steak for 2 hours in covered container and refrigerate. Turn or stir occasionally for even marination.

Sprinkle flour into a shallow pan. Remove the meat from the marinade and dredge the slices in flour. Shake off any excess flour.

Heat a frying pan over medium-high heat. Add some vegetable oil to lightly coat the pan and sauté the beef until nicely browned; this should take about 1½ to 2 minutes on each side. Serve immediately.

Roast Beef

Yield: Serving size varies

This delicious recipe for roast beef never fails to please. It's also perfect for those cooks on the go: simply place the roast in the oven for half an hour before heading out of the house in the morning (be sure to turn the oven off before leaving); upon returning, just turn the oven on 30 minutes before dinner and voilà!, dinner is served.

**Beef rib or cross rib roast, any size (allow 4-6 oz. cooked portion/
person)
Hawaiian salt to taste
Freshly ground pepper to taste**

Leave roast out of refrigerator and let stand at room temperature about 2 hours. Salt and pepper to taste; place on rack in shallow roasting plan lined with aluminum foil for easy cleaning. Roast at 400°F for 60 minutes. Turn oven off and leave roast in oven to rest minimum of 3 hours. DO NOT OPEN OVEN DOOR. 20 minutes before serving, turn oven on at 300°F and roast for 20 minutes. Serve with au jus or gravy of your choice.

Tip: If using packaged au jus or gravy mix, follow package directions.

Oven Pot Roast

Yield: About 8 servings

When entertaining, a dish that doesn't require much attention is welcome as it allows the hosts time to attend to guests and conversation. This oven pot roast is just such a dish. Once in the oven, it requires little attention and the clean up is easy, too. —MURIEL MIURA

4 pounds pot roast (chuck, round or rump)
¾ cup water
1 package (1¾ oz.) dry onion soup mix
4 medium carrots, cut in 1-inch pieces
4 medium potatoes, quartered
1 cup celery, cut in ½-inch pieces
1 large onion, wedged

Trim fat from meat; place on large piece of heavy duty aluminum foil in roasting pan. Mix water and dry onion soup mix in bowl; pour over meat. Bring ends of foil over meat and seal in "drug-store" wrap. Roast at 350°F for 2 hours. Open foil carefully; add vegetables. Cook additional 30 to 45 minutes or until vegetables are done and meat is tender.

Paniolo Rib-Eye Steak

Yield: 4 to 5 servings

If you live on Maui be sure to use beef from Maui Cattle Company which was started in 2002, by a group of independent ranchers who wanted to market their free-range, naturally raised, local meat under a recognizable brand name. —TYLUN PANG

2 (16- to 18-ounce) bone-in rib-eye steaks

Steak Rub:

1 teaspoon chopped garlic
1 teaspoon chopped parsley
½ teaspoon dried chili pepper flakes
2 tablespoons turbinado sugar (Maui raw sugar)
2 tablespoons Hawaiian 'alaea salt

Chop the garlic and parsley. Mix all ingredients for the rub and apply it to the steaks.

Grill steaks about 4 to 5 minutes on each side (or to your taste). You'll get the best flavor if you grill over a kiawe wood fire.

Let the steak rest for a few minutes before serving.

Shoyu Short Ribs Pipikaula-Style

Yield: 6 to 8 servings

Upcountry Maui has been cattle country since the early 1800s, when cattle first came to the islands and Hawaiian cowboys or paniolos, learned to ride, rope, and herd. Lacking refrigerators, early ranchers preserved beef by sundrying it and turning it into jerky. Hawaiian-kine jerky is called pipikaula, or beef string. It's usually spicier and softer than mainland jerky.

This innovative short rib recipe treats the ribs pipikaula style. The ribs are marinated and then slowly oven dried. Store them in the refrigerator and briefly fry or broil before eating. —TYLUN PANG

4 pounds short ribs, sliced ¾-inch thick

Marinade:

2 teaspoons ginger peeled and grated
1 teaspoon minced garlic
½ teaspoon crushed dried red chili peppers, or to taste
1 cup soy sauce
½ cup sugar
¼ cup mirin

Cut the short ribs into individual ribs and then cut each rib into chunks ¾-inch long. Prepare the ginger and garlic per the instructions in the ingredients list.

Mix all the marinade ingredients in a large container with a lid. Add the short ribs. Cover and refrigerate for 2 hours. Turn the rib chunks frequently, so that they marinate evenly.

Preheat the oven to 165°F. Remove the ribs from the container, letting any excess marinade drain off. Set them on a wire rack in a foil-lined broiler pan or baking pan. The sliced ribs should be well-separated; if they touch, they will not dry evenly. Dry the meat in the preheated oven for 3 hours. Turn the ribs over and dry for another 3 hours.

Remove the ribs from the oven and let them cool completely. Wrap them well and store them in your refrigerator. They will keep for 2 weeks.

Before serving, pan-fry the short ribs in a little vegetable oil over medium-high heat, until they are brown on both sides. You can also broil them over a kiawe charcoal fire.

Chinese Five-Spice Boneless Short Ribs

Courtesy of Chef Becky Speere

Yield: 4 servings

This recipe is wonderful made with just any short ribs, but it's better than wonderful when prepared with locally raised Maui Cattle Company beef. It's a Crock-Pot recipe that requires a ten-hour cooking time. Start it early in the morning for a delicious, no-fuss dinner. If you don't want to get up at the crack of dawn to make this for dinner, cook overnight, put in the refrigerator, and reheat. Stews often improve when they are allowed to sit before being reheated.

4 pounds short ribs
1 cup sliced green onion (½-inch slices)
3 medium cloves garlic, thinly sliced
2 tablespoons ginger, peeled and thinly sliced
½ cup flour
2 tablespoons oil
½ cup hoisin sauce
½ cup soy sauce
½ cup Chinese rice wine OR dry sherry
½ cup Maui raw sugar
1 teaspoon Chinese five-spice
½ teaspoon ground white pepper

Approximately 2 to 3 pieces of boneless short ribs would be the equivalent of 4 pounds. Prepare the green onions, garlic, and ginger per the instructions in the ingredients list.

Lightly flour the short ribs. Heat the 2 tablespoons of oil in a large frying pan over medium-high heat; brown the ribs.

Put the short ribs in a Crock-Pot. Add the rest of the recipe ingredients, including the prepared onion, garlic, and ginger. Mix well. Cook for 10 hours on the Crock-Pot's medium setting.

Presentation:

Chef Becky Speere likes to serve these ribs over hot rice, with Maui-grown pickled vegetables on the side.

Burgundy Braised Short Ribs

Chef Russell Siu, 3660 On the Rise

Yield: 6 servings

Burgundy Short Ribs is one of Executive Chef Russell Siu's popular dishes at 3660 On the Rise. The recipe is delicious, the presentation is beautiful, and the preparation is simple, too—especially since Chef Siu has been gracious enough to share his recipe below!

½ cup oil
6 (3-bone) short ribs, 2-inch thick (cut between bone)
½ cup small diced bacon
1 tablespoon minced shallots
5 cloves garlic, peeled
1 teaspoon fresh thyme
½ teaspoon rosemary
3 cups burgundy wine
3 quarts beef broth or stock
1 cup small diced carrots
1 cup small diced onions
3 cups mushrooms, quartered
½ cup caramel sauce
1½ cups pearl onions
¾ cup unsalted butter
¾ cup flour
Salt and pepper to taste

In a brazier add oil and short ribs. Brown over medium high heat until ribs are nice and brown. Add bacon, shallots, garlic, thyme, rosemary and mix. Simmer for about 4 minutes; add burgundy wine. Simmer another 4 minutes and then add beef stock, carrots and onions. Cover and simmer for about 1½ hours over low heat. Add mushrooms and simmer until short ribs are tender. Add caramel and pearl onions; simmer for about 6 minutes. Mix together butter and flour until smooth; add slowly to short ribs, stirring constantly, for about 15 minutes. Season with salt and pepper.

Pineapple Grill's Kalbi Short Ribs

Chef Ryan Luckey, Pineapple Grill, Kapalua

Yield: 4 servings

"Kalbi Short Ribs has been a local favorite for decades. We took a different spin on the classic Azeka's Ribs, using our own style of the Korean kalbi sauce. We perfected the slow cooking of our short rib, using lemongrass, kaffir lime leaf, fresh ginger, garlic, and star anise to bring a distinct flavor. The rich Kalbi demi-glace is a sauce that needs balance, the perfect levels of sweet and savory are key.

I prepared this dish at the Maui Culinary Academy's fundraiser when I was a guest chef. You can use boneless short ribs if you like. I recommend the bone-in ribs, which have more taste. Serve these ribs with Maui Gold Pineapple Salsa (recipe follows)." —CHEF RYAN LUCKEY

4 pounds of short ribs OR 4 (2½ inch cut) kosher short ribs, bone-in
3 medium-sized stalks celery, chopped
1 medium-sized onion, peeled and chopped
1 medium-sized carrot, peeled and chopped
2 ounces fresh ginger, roughly chopped
4 stalks lemongrass, chopped
6 cloves garlic, crushed

Salt and pepper to taste
Kosher salt and freshly ground pepper
2 tablespoons olive oil; more if needed
8 kaffir lime leaves
1 teaspoon coriander seeds
1 teaspoon whole black pepper
9 whole star anise
3 quarts beef or veal stock OR beef bouillon

Kalbi Sauce:

½ cup chopped green onion
1 tablespoon peeled and minced fresh ginger
2 cups water OR stock left over after the ribs have been cooked

2 cups granulated sugar (less if you prefer a stronger soy sauce flavor)
2 cups Aloha low-salt soy sauce
1 tablespoon sesame oil
1 tablespoon toasted white sesame seeds

Cornstarch Slurry:

2 tablespoons cornstarch
3 tablespoons cold water

(continued on page 108)

Roughly chop the celery, onion, carrot, ginger, lemongrass, and garlic per the ingredient list. These vegetables are going to flavor the broth in which the ribs are cooked; you are not going to serve them.

Season ribs with a nice dusting of kosher salt and black pepper. Add 1 tablespoon of the olive oil to a large pot over medium-high heat. When the oil is hot, add the ribs. Sear each side for about 30 to 45 seconds, or until the ribs are golden-brown. You may need to do this in several batches; don't crowd the pot, or the meat will stew rather than brown. Add more oil if needed to keep the ribs from sticking. Remove the cooked meat and set it to one side.

Keep the heat under the pot at medium-high; add another tablespoon of olive oil. Put the chopped vegetables and the lime leaves, coriander, black pepper, and star anise in the pot and sauté for about 1 to 2 minutes, or until the vegetables have wilted. Add more oil if needed to keep the food from sticking. Put the ribs back into the pot and add the beef stock or bouillon. If the liquid doesn't cover the beef, add water until the meat is covered.

Bring the ribs and broth to a simmer; turn the heat to low and cook for another 2 hours. The meat should be tender and falling off the bone. If it isn't, cook a little longer.

When the ribs are cooked, take out of the stock. If you don't want to bother with the stock, you can discard it. However, you will probably want to filter the stock through a sieve, removing all the vegetable and spice remnants and leaving a highly-seasoned beef broth.

Remove the cooked meat from the bones and discard the bones. You may want to trim off any remaining rib cartilage at this time. Set the meat aside to rest and cool for 10 minutes.

While the meat is resting, make your kalbi sauce. Prepare the chopped green onion and minced ginger per the instructions in the ingredients list. Put the water or stock, sugar, soy sauce, sesame oil, and minced ginger in a small saucepan and bring to a simmer. In another bowl, mix the cornstarch and cold water to make smooth paste. Stir this slurry into the sauce. The sauce will thicken almost instantly. Take the sauce off the heat and add the chopped green onions and the sesame seeds. Check the consistency of the sauce and if it is too thick, add a little water.

Pour the kalbi sauce into a large pan and add the meat from the ribs. Bring the mixture to a simmer; reduce the heat slightly and cook over low heat for about 5 minutes. The meat should be coated with the thick, spicy sauce.

Maui Gold Pineapple Salsa

Chef Ryan Luckey, Pineapple Grill, Kapalua

Yield: 6 cups

"I like to heat up this sauce with the chilies in Sriracha sauce or sambal paste. But ... not everyone likes it hot, so feel free to leave out the fiery ingredients."

1 whole pineapple, peeled, cored, diced (¼-inch dice)
½ cup diced red bell pepper (¼-inch dice)
¼ cup diced red onion (¼-inch dice)
1 tablespoon chopped cilantro
2 or 3 tablespoons lime juice (about 1 average lime)
Sriracha sauce OR sambal paste, to taste (optional)
Sea salt to taste

Combine all ingredients. Mix well and taste to correct seasonings as needed.

Beef Shank Laulau

Chef Perry Bateman, Mama's Fish House, Pāʻia

Yield: 1 laulau

"Being Hawaiian, the love of Hawaiian food is in my koko (blood). One of my favorite dishes is laulau. Laulau is a leaf bundle in which we bake pork, beef, chicken, or butterfish, together with ʻulu (breadfruit), sweet potato, or kalo (taro). We use ti and kalo leaves for wrapping. The traditional way to make laulau is to bake them in an imu (earth oven). These days, imu are only for special occasions. The rest of the time, we make the laulau in a steamer or a pressure cooker. We lose the lovely smoky imu taste, but the laulau are still ʻono.

I experimented until I figured out a way to make the best beef laulau ever. Secret? Beef shank, which is full of flavor but low in fat, AND thin slices of fat from a beef roast. You can get the fat from your butcher, or save it if you're trimming prime rib before cooking it for your family. Nestle the fat next to the beef shank and cook. The fat melts and soaks into the meat, bringing out all the flavor.

That's the secret of my special laulau. Just between us, OK? No give away the secret now!"

A pressure cooker dramatically reduces the laulau cooking time. If you love laulau and make them often, consider investing in a pressure cooker.

> ½ cups sweet potatoes OR ʻulu (breadfruit) OR cooked taro
> 1 pound beef shank (bone in, whole)
> ¼ cup beef fat
> 6 ti leaves (you'll only use 4 leaves, but buy extra in case you have problems removing the ribs)
> 4 to 5 large lūʻau (kalo) leaves
> Hawaiian salt

Remove the stiff ribs from the back of the ti leaves. There's no need to steam the leaves, as you are cooking the laulau in a steamer. Do save a couple of the stems; you'll need them to tie up the laulau.

To prepare the lūʻau leaves, remove any thick, fibrous ribs or veins. Cut off the stem. You can chop up the stem and put it inside the laulau, or you can save it for stew.

To assemble the laulau:

Lay down 2 leaves, parallel to each other. Lay 2 leaves across the first 2, forming a large, fat cross. Arrange the lūʻau leaves in a wheel, tips pointing outward.

Put the beef fat in the middle of the lūʻau leaves. Sprinkle the fat with a little Hawaiian salt. Put the beef shank on top of the fat and sprinkle with salt again. Put the sweet potato, }ulu, or kalo on top of the beef shank.

Wrap the lūʻau leaves around the ingredients, as if you were making a burrito. Pull up the ends of the ti leaves, forming a bag. Tie the bag with 1 or 2 ti leaf stems.

If you have a tiered steamer, put the laulau in a pan to catch the drippings, place in the top tier, and steam for 4 to 5 hours. Keep an eye on the water; don't let the steamer boil dry.

If you have a pressure cooker, put the pan on a stand inside the cooker, add water, seal, and cook for approximately 1 hour.

When the laulau is done, pour the drippings into a container or a fat skimmer. Let the fat rise to the top and skim it off. Save it, don't throw it out.

Unwrap the laulau and discard the ti leaves. Taste a bit of the laulau. Does it need more seasoning? Add salt and some of the skimmed fat if necessary.

Ginger Hoisin Hibachi Rack of Haleakalā Lamb

Yield: 4 to 6 servings

When you are grilling whole lamb racks, make sure your fire isn't too hot. If it's too hot, the lamb will burn on the outside and remain raw on the inside. Light your coals on your barbecue, then let the fire cool down until your coals become lightly covered with ash. This should be an ideal temperature to begin grilling your lamb. Ask your butcher for Frenched racks with the chine bone removed. —TYLUN PANG

2 lamb racks, approximately 14 to 16 ounces each

Marinade:

2 tablespoons finely chopped green onion
2 tablespoons peeled and minced ginger
1 cup hoisin sauce
1 cup mirin
½ cup oyster sauce
½ cup water
¼ cup soy sauce
1 teaspoon sambal oelek (Indonesian chili paste)

Chop the green onion and ginger per the ingredients list; mix all the ingredients for the marinade in a large baking dish.

Trim all but a thin layer of fat from the lamb. Score the fat side of each rack in a crosshatch pattern. Put the racks in the baking dish and coat with the marinade. Cover the dish with a lid or with plastic wrap. Refrigerate at least 8 hours or overnight. Turn racks occasionally for even marination.

Fire up your hibachi or charcoal grill until the coals are ready. Grill the lamb racks over medium-heat coals for 5 to 6 minutes on each side. Test the meat with an instant-read meat thermometer to be sure that it's fully cooked; the thermometer, inserted into the center (but not touching bone), should read 120°F for medium-rare or 125°F for medium.

When the meat is done, remove the meat from the grill and cover it with an aluminum foil tent. Let it rest for 5 minutes before slicing it into chops and serving.

Seafood satisfies the most discriminate palate with its hearty aroma and robust flavor. Surrounded by the ocean and with a strong fishing culture, the day's catches from local fishermen offer a wide array of ingredients fresh off the boat. Here is a complete assortment of tantalizing recipes that will bring to your table the delicate textures of ʻahi, ʻōpakapaka, aku, mahimahi, ono, butterfish and monchong.

Shake up standard weeknight fare by breaking out the fryer for those oh-so-delicious Island fish fillets. Reel in easy dinners with mouth-watering Misoyaki Butterfish or Fried Curried Mahimahi and more!

MAIN DISHES
SEAFOOD

'Ahi Cakes with Roasted Sweet Corn Relish

Executive Chef Goran V. Streng, Tango Contemporary Café

Yield: 2 servings

Göran Streng is best known for his tenure as executive chef at the Hawaii Prince Hotel, where he presided over the resort's massive buffet and many fine-dining restaurants. A few years ago, he set off on his own, starting the catering company ScandinAsian Culinary Concepts, which merges his background—he is a native of Finland—with the foods and flavors of his adopted home. These 'ahi cakes provide a fresh take on the crab cake, spiced with chili, tangy with lime juice, and topped with a sweet blend of corn, papaya and veggies.

'Ahi Cakes:

- 1 pound fresh 'ahi, finely chopped
- ½ cup diced onion
- ¼ cup minced green onion
- 2 tablespoons chopped cilantro
- 2 teaspoons chili paste (Sambal Oelek preferred)
- 2 teaspoons lime juice
- 2 tablespoons Worcestershire sauce
- Salt and pepper to taste

Sweet Corn Relish:

- 2 pieces sweet roasted corn on the cob
- 1 cup diced firm ripe papaya
- ¼ cup diced red bell pepper
- ¼ cup diced green bell pepper
- ¼ cup diced sweet onion
- ¼ cup Balsamic vinegar
- ½ cup olive oil
- 2 tablespoons minced cilantro
- Salt and pepper to taste

Combine all ingredients for 'Ahi Cakes in a bowl and mix well. Use a small ice cream disher to portion out the mix, directly into a hot sauté pan with some oil. Cook for about one minute on each side. Serve hot with Sweet Corn Relish.

To prepare relish, cut corn off the husk into a bowl and mix with the other ingredients. Serve over or on the side of 'Ahi Cakes.

Tempura

Yield: Varies

Tempura ranks among the great dishes of Hawai'i, if not the world, and is known throughout for its unmatched delicacy. Tempura was introduced centuries ago to Japan by the Portuguese and Spanish who established missions in southern Japan. It is a food dipped in batter then deep fried and served with a dipping sauce mixed with grated daikon. If you prefer a lighter batter, use #2. —MURIEL MIURA

Batter #1 (Yields 1¾ cups):

½ cup flour
½ cup cornstarch
½ cup ice-cold water
1 egg, beaten

Batter #2 (Yields 2¼ cups):

⅔ cup cake flour
⅓ cup cornstarch
1 cup ice-cold water
1 egg, beaten

Sift together dry ingredients; set aside. In a separate bowl add water to egg; stir well. Add dry ingredients all at once to egg-water mixture; stir briefly, just enough to combine mixture. The batter will be lumpy. Do not overmix. Heat oil to 365 to 375°F. Dip cleaned and prepared seafood or vegetables into batter and deep fry in oil until lightly browned. Drain on absorbant paper and serve with tempura sauce while hot.

Suggested tempura ingredients:

Vegetables: Asparagus spears, burdock root, lotus root, bamboo shoots, ginko nuts on skewers, sweet potato slices, carrot slices, green beans, bell pepper slices, sweet onion slices, broccoli crowns, cauliflower, zucchini slices, mushrooms, shiso (beefsteak plant leaves), parsley, nori (laver), pumpkin slices, okra, eggplant, etc.

Seafoods: Fish fillet (mahi, 'ahi, sole, sea bass, etc.), shrimp (shelled and cleaned with tails on), calamari, etc.

**Tempura Sauce #1
 (Yields 1½ cups):**

1 cup water
½ teaspoon dashi-no-moto
¼ cup mirin (sweet rice wine)
¼ cup soy sauce
1 tablespoon sugar

**Tempura Sauce #2
 (Yields 2 cups):**

1 piece (5-inch) dashi konbu
2 cups boiling water
½ cup dried bonito flakes
2 teaspoons soy sauce
½ teaspoon salt
½ teaspoon sugar

Condiments for Sauce:

½ cup grated daikon (white radish)
1 tablespoon minced green onion

Tempura Sauce #1: Combine all ingredients and bring to a boil. Cool. Add condiments to serve.

Tempura Sauce #2: Add konbu to boiling water; cook 10 minutes. Add bonito flakes; cook 3 minutes; strain. Add remaining ingredients and bring to a boil. Cool. Add condiments to serve.

∾ *Tips for great tempura:*

- *Use ice-cold water*
- *Keep batter chilled*
- *Do not overmix batter; leave lumps*
- *Coat food lightly with batter*
- *Prepare small quantity of batter at a time*
- *Cook small quantities at a time*
- *Serve hot*

Ginger Crusted 'Ōpakapaka Plum Chili Sauce

Chef Russell Siu, 3660 On the Rise

Yield: 4 servings

Russell Siu's 3660 On the Rise is an oasis of chic in one of O'ahu's oldest neighborhoods, Kaimukī. But it's not a fussy, fancy place, and Russell's style reflects a simplicity of form that still manages to be elegant on the plate. In this dish, fillets of 'ōpakapaka (snapper) are crusted with panko heavily seasoned with ginger.

4 pieces (6 ounces each) 'ōpakapaka fillets
⅛ cup gated ginger
⅛ cup finely chopped green onions
⅛ cup finely chopped cilantro

1½ cups panko (Japanese bread crumbs)
⅛ cup vegetable oil or clarified butter
Kosher salt and black pepper to taste

Plum Chili Sauce:

1 cup plum wine
½ cup rice vinegar
Juice of ½ lime
1 tablespoon chopped scallion
1 tablespoon chopped fresh ginger

1 tablespoon chopped shallots
1½ tablespoons chili sauce (Lingham preferred)
6 tablespoons heavy cream
¾ cup unsalted butter
Kosher salt and black pepper to taste

Mix together ginger, green onions, cilantro and panko. Season fish fillets with salt and pepper. Press one side of fillet onto panko mixture making sure that the crust evenly coats fillet. Pan fry, panko side down first, in a hot pan with oil or butter until golden brown. Turn, continue cooking until fish is cooked through (about 5 minutes over medium heat). Drain on absorbent paper.

To prepare sauce, combine plum wine, rice vinegar, lime juice, scallion, shallots, ginger, shallots and chili sauce; reduce by half the volume. Add heavy cream and reduce until cream starts to thicken. Whisk in butter slowly until all of the butter is incorporated. Strain through a fine sieve and season with salt and pepper.

To serve, ladle sauce onto center of plate and place cooked fillet on top of sauce. Garnish with sprig of cilantro.

Pan-Fried Teriyaki Salmon

Yield: 4 servings

Teriyaki sauce can add a wonderful flavor to nearly any meat. That is especially true of this recipe when the sauce is drizzled over moist, pan-fried fish fillet.

This is also the perfect dish to serve a large, hungry crowd—just place the salmon on a baking pan lined with greased foil and bake as many pieces of fish that will fit on the pan all at once.

4 (4 oz.) salmon steaks or fillets
Canola oil

Teriyaki Sauce:

¼ cup brown sugar, packed
¼ cup soy sauce
⅓ cup mirin (sweet rice wine)
1 teaspoon grated fresh ginger

Combine Teriyaki Sauce ingredients in saucepan; heat until sugar dissolves; set aside.

Pat-dry salmon pieces with damp paper towel. Pan-fry fish in hot oil until browned and opaque on both sides. Brush Teriyaki Sauce on salmon; plate then drizzle more sauce just before serving.

Aku Burgers

Yield: 12 burgers

Many Japanese plantation workers left the plantations to start their own businesses—sometimes in rural areas, sometimes in the larger towns. Hilo, the largest town on the Big Island, had its own Japan-town, known as Shinmachi (New Town). Shinmachi, alas, was totally destroyed in the 1946 tsunami, which killed 159 people throughout the Islands and 96 in Hilo alone—many of them were from Shinmachi, which was exposed to the full force of the enormous waves. Today, that land is a public park.

Hilo has always been home to many fishermen. In the old days, fishermen got the best price for 'ahi, the large bigeye or yellowfin tuna. When they caught aku, the small skipjack tuna, they gave them away. Thrifty Shinmachi residents used to make burgers from aku. This recipe was handed down from those living in Shinmachi from 1920-1946.

1 pound aku, all bones removed and chopped
1½ teaspoons salt
2 tablespoons sugar
½ cup finely chopped onions
½ cup slivered gobo (burdock)
1 large egg

Chop the fish until it is the consistency of ground meat. Add the salt, sugar, onions, gobo and continue to chop until all ingredients are mixed together and are finely chopped. Add egg, mix well.

Add enough canola oil to a frying pan to coat the bottom. Make one patty, approximately ½-inch thick and 2 inches in diameter. Fry one, taste. Add salt or sugar to adjust flavors, then make up the rest of the patties. Fry the patties and drain on a paper towel before serving.

Fried Curried Mahimahi

Yield: 4 servings

Once, years ago, I was hosting a dinner for several very important guests. I felt that it was imperative that I serve them something that represented Hawai'i and the variety of exotic flavors found here. After testing numerous dishes, I decided upon this recipe for mahimahi. It turned out to be a winning dish! —Muriel Miura

1 pound mahimahi fillet,
   cut into serving slices and
   scored
1 egg, beaten
1 cup panko
1 quart salad oil for frying

Marinade:

1 tablespoon sugar
1 teaspoon salt
1 tablespoon mirin (sweet rice
   wine)
2 teaspoons curry powder
2 tablespoons cornstarch
1 tablespoon soy sauce

Combine marinade ingredients; mix well and marinate fish fillets 30 minutes. Dip fish in egg and dredge in panko. Deep fry in oil heated to 365°F until golden brown on both sides, about 3 minutes. Drain on absorbent paper. Serve hot.

Macadamia Nut-Crusted Mahimahi with Olowalu Nui Tomato and Ginger

Yield: 4 servings

It's our responsibility to support our local fishermen and farmers. I always use fish from Maui waters and local produce whenever possible—like Olowalu tomatoes, which are fresher and sweeter because they are kept on the vines longer. Adding pickled ginger adds a new twist.
—TYLUN PANG

2 tablespoons melted butter
4 (5-ounce) mahimahi fillets
Salt and pepper to taste

Nut Crust:

½ cup finely chopped macadamia nuts
½ teaspoon chopped parsley
½ cup panko (Japanese-style bread crumbs)
½ teaspoon paprika

Tomato Ginger Sauce:

1 cup seeded and diced (¼-inch) tomato
¼ cup finely diced Maui onion
1 tablespoon finely sliced green onions
2 teaspoons finely minced pickled ginger
2 tablespoons olive oil
4 tablespoons butter
Salt and pepper to taste

Preheat the oven to 400°F.

To make the nut crust, chop the nuts and parsley per the instructions in the ingredients list. Mix the nuts, parsley, panko, and paprika in a shallow pan and set aside.

To make the sauce, prepare the tomato, onion, green onions, and ginger per the ingredients list. Heat the olive oil in a sauté pan over medium heat; add the chopped onion and cook until soft. Add the diced tomatoes and pickled ginger and cook for 1 to 2 minutes. Whisk in the butter. When it has melted, turn off the heat under the pan and add the green onions. Season with salt and pepper to taste. Cover the sauce to retain heat.

Melt the butter in a small saucepan or the microwave. Season the mahimahi fillets with salt and pepper. Coat the fillets with the nut crust mixture. Put the fillets in a baking pan and drizzle with the melted butter. Bake the fillets in the 400°F oven until the crust is nicely browned, about 10 minutes.

Serve the cooked fish on top of the finished tomato and ginger sauce.

Crisp Pan-Fried Ono with Yuzu-Soy Vinaigrette

Roy's Restaurant
Roy Yamaguchi, Chef/Owner

Yield: 4 servings

Roy Yamaguchi is Hawai'i's most successful restaurateur, with three dozen restaurants across the country and in Asia. He was also Hawai'i's first winner of the prestigious James Beard Foundation Award, proving that his culinary skills match his business expertise. Roy calls his style "Hawaiian Fusion," grounding himself in the islands, but allowing him free reign to experiment with the flavors of the world. This dish relies on Asian tastes of sake, ginger, yuzu (a Japanese citrus) and soy sauce. The ingredient list is intimidating, but once you have all the fixings together, the technique is not difficult. The fish, ono (also called wahoo), is simply marinated and fried.

4 (7-ounces each) ono fillets
4 cups canola oil for frying
4 large egg whites
1 cup cornstarch for dusting
Salt and freshly ground black pepper

Marinade:

½ cup soy sauce
¼ cup freshly squeezed lemon juice
3 tablespoons sake (rice wine)
1½ tablespoons ginger juice
3 tablespoons sugar
¼ cup finely sliced scallions (including green parts)

Yuzu-Soy Vinaigrette:

½ cup yuzu juice*
½ cup soy sauce
2 tablespoons olive oil
2 tablespoons peanut oil
2 tablespoons sugar
¼ cup grated fresh ginger
2 tablespoons minced onion chives or regular chives

To prepare the Marinade, combine the soy sauce, lemon juice, sake and ginger juice in a bowl. Add the sugar and whisk until sugar dissolves, then whisk in the scallions. Add the ono and marinate for 15 to 20 minutes, turning once.

While the ono is marinating, prepare the Yuzu-Soy Vinaigrette. Combine yuzu, soy sauce, olive oil and peanut oil in a bowl; add sugar and whisk until sugar dissolves. Whisk in ginger and chives; set aside.

Heat canola oil to 375°F in deep fryer or large, heavy saucepan. Whisk egg whites in a bowl until frothy. Remove ono from marinade and dip into egg whites; dust with cornstarch and season with salt and pepper to taste. Fry ono in hot oil for 3 to 4 minutes or until golden brown; drain on absorbent paper and arrange on warmed plates. Drizzle the vinaigrette around the ono and serve.

*Note: ¼ cup fresh lemon juice mixed with ¼ cup orange juice may be substituted for yuzu juice.

Imitation Crab Patties with Tofu

Natsue Kametani, Kula

Yield: 6 servings

This recipe is one that appeals to just about everybody.

1 (14-ounce) block of firm tofu, well drained
1 (10-ounce) package imitation crab
2 eggs
¼ cup mayonnaise
¼ cup string beans, chopped
¼ cup Kula onions, chopped
3 tablespoons green onions, chopped
¼ cup carrots, grated
Seasoned salt and pepper to taste

Mix all ingredients together. Shape into patties and fry in skillet on medium heat.

Wok-Seared Monchong with Black Bean Sauce

Yield: 4 servings

Chinese chefs use douchi, fermented black beans, to add a piquant touch to many dishes. You can buy black bean sauces in bottles at the supermarket but for the best taste, I recommend that you make your own sauce from scratch. In this recipe, the sauce complements some wok-fried monchong. If you like the taste, you may want to try your homemade sauce with other fish dishes or with Chinese-style spareribs. This is dad's, Yun Young Pang's, version of black bean sauce. You can substitute a soft textured white fish. Monchong can only be found in Hawaiian waters. Its high oil content preserves moisture and offers a unique deep buttery flavor. —TYLUN PANG

> **4 (5-ounce) monchong fillets**
> **Salt and pepper to season**
> **4 tablespoons flour**
> **2 tablespoons oil**

> Black Bean Sauce:
>
> **2 tablespoons fermented black beans, rinsed and drained**
> **1 clove garlic, minced**
> **1 teaspoon minced ginger**
> **¼ teaspoon red chili pepper flakes**
> **1 tablespoon oil**
> **¾ cup chicken stock**
> **2 tablespoons oyster sauce**
> **1 teaspoon sugar**
> **½ teaspoon salt**

> Cornstarch Slurry:
>
> **2 teaspoons cornstarch**
> **1 tablespoon cold water**

> **1 tablespoon finely sliced green onions, for garnish**

To make the sauce, rinse and drain the fermented black beans. Mince the garlic and ginger. Heat the oil in a small saucepan over medium heat; add the black beans, garlic, ginger, and chili flakes and sauté until fragrant. Add the chicken stock, oyster sauce, sugar, and salt. Raise the heat slightly and bring the mixture to a boil. Turn the heat down to medium-low. Mix the cornstarch and water into a smooth paste. Add the cornstarch slurry to the sauce and stir until the sauce thickens. Remove the sauce from the heat and cover to retain heat.

Season monchong fillets with salt and pepper to your taste. Dredge fish in the flour; shake off any excess. Heat the oil in a large frying pan over medium-high heat. When the oil is hot, add the fish and cook for 3 minutes on each side, or until the fish is cooked. It will no longer be opaque and will be starting to stiffen. Fish continues to cook even after you remove it from the pan, so it is best to slightly undercook the fish and let it finish cooking on the plate.

Place fish on a serving platter and ladle black bean sauce over the top. Garnish with the sliced green onions.

Misoyaki Butterfish

Kyo-ya

Yield: 10 to 12 servings

Miso Butterfish is an oh-so-traditional Japanese dish that can be found on humble teishoku trays, as well as the fine china of the fanciest restaurants.

Famed chef Nobu Matsuhisa brought the dish to the Western world as Black Cod with Miso, but he was building on the simple broiled fish that his mother probably served. What distinguishes this dish is the combination of varieties of miso, or the additional flavors in the marinade. This version adds sake kasu, a grainy byproduct of sake-making, to add a boozy touch to the usual sugar, soy sauce and miso.

5 to 6 pounds butterfish fillets, cut into serving pieces

Marinade:

¾ pound sake kasu (rice wine dregs)
3 cups granulated sugar
1 cup soy sauce
1 cup sake (rice wine)
2 pounds red miso

Placed thawed butterfish in colander to drain excess water overnight in refrigerator.

Combine sake kasu, sugar, and soy sauce; mix well. Stir in red miso and mix to blend ingredients thoroughly. Place fish fillets in marinade and marinate, covered in refrigerator for three days. Rinse off marinade from fish and place on rack to broil. (It is very important to place fish on rack as lots of liquid and oil will drip.) Turn fish three to four times to avoid burning while broiling, about 5 to 6 minutes. A toaster oven may be used to broil a small quantity.

To finish, brush your favorite teriyaki sauce thickened with potato starch on the butterfish.

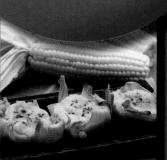

SALADS, SOUPS, AND SIDES

Hawai'i's salads, soups, and sides bring together succulent meats, exotic vegetables, and savory goodness to complement and can even rival any entrée on the table. From comforting to cool and crisp, our salads, soups and sides are the "feel-good" foods that add color and zest to a meal as well as making it more interesting and balanced.

Soup recipes range from nostalgic classics to cultural favorites to innovative creations with a multicultural twist. Salad recipes encompass all the flavors from sweet to spicy and taste even better when using locally grown produce from farmers markets. These recipes are sophisticated offerings that can stand on their own and when combined, can even be enjoyed as a whole meal. They are our comfort foods that soothe the soul on a rainy day or sate a hearty appetite after a long day at the beach.

Crunchy Salmon Salad

Leonora Takayama

Yield: 6 servings

Pipinola shoots should perhaps be called chayote shoots, as they are the shoots harvested from the plant more commonly known as chayote or mirliton. You can usually buy them at farmers' markets.

This recipe for pipinola shoots was created by Leonora Takayama, of Hilo. It won first place in the salad division at the first annual Tomato Recipe Contest, sponsored by Hāmākua Country Spring Farms.

1 package (12 ounce) ready-cubed salted salmon (lomi), rinsed and drained

½ pound (approximately 1 bunch) pipinola shoots

½ pound string beans, cut at a slant, each piece 1¼ inches long

1 young pipinola (chayote) fruit, approximately 5 inches long

1½ cups diced Roma tomatoes (½-inch dice) (approximately 5 large tomatoes)

1 cup diced sweet onion (½-inch dice) (approximately 1 onion)

Sauce:

1 tablespoon patis (fish sauce)
1 tablespoon sweet chili sauce
1 tablespoon water
2 tablespoons brown sugar
1 teaspoon sesame oil

To prepare the sauce: Mix together and set aside.

To prepare the pipinola shoots: Use only the tender parts of the shoots. Cut them into ¼-inch slices.

To prepare the pipinola (chayote) fruit: Trim off the top and bottom of the fruit. Peel. Cut the fruit into quarters, lengthwise, and trim out the seed in the middle. Cut across the quarters to make ¼-inch slices. Soak them in cold water to rinse off the sticky sap.

To prepare the salad: In a large pot, bring water to a rolling boil. Parboil the pipinola shoots, string beans, and pipinola. Parboil each kind of vegetable separately, as they all require different cooking times. Pipinola shoots: 1 minute; string beans: 2 minutes; pipinola: 3 minutes.

When the vegetables are just tender, put them in cold water to prevent them from cooking any further. The retained heat in the vegetables might otherwise make them mushy.

Mix all the ingredients in a large bowl. Marinate the salad for a minimum of 1 hour; overnight might be better. Serve when chilled.

Salmon Skin Tofu Salad

Chef Hideaki "Santa" Miyoshi, Tokkuri-Tei Restaurant

Yield: 4 servings

Hideaki Miyoshi is known for his playful way with sushi and other Japanese specialties served at his small Kapahulu restaurant, Tokkuri-Tei. His nickname of "Santa," might have come from that, although the chef himself says he used to be heavy and round, like Santa. This salad calls for grilling the skin with a very thin layer of flesh, then serving the crisp and tasty result over a tofu salad.

1 whole fresh Atlantic salmon
Salt
8 ounces onion, thinly sliced, rinsed
   and drained
4 ounces kaiware (radish sprouts)
3 tablespoons mayonnaise
1 teaspoon fresh ginger, grated
1 teaspoon momiji oroshi (Japanese
   chili paste with grated daikon)
3 tablespoons masago (smelt eggs)
2 blocks (12 ounces each) silky or
   soft tofu (soybean curd), sliced into
   halves
4 ounces Nalo or garden greens,
   washed and drained
Kizami nori (shredded seaweed)

To prepare salmon, fillet the whole salmon. Spread salt evenly on a sheet pan. Place the salmon fillet, skin side down, on pan and cover top of salmon with more salt. Let stand for 2 to 3 hours, depending on size of salmon, to cure. Rinse salt off and dry with paper towel. Cut off skin, leaving about ⅛-inch salmon flesh attached. Save the salmon fillet for later use as sashimi. Grill the salmon skin in a pan until crispy, chop into bite-size pieces, and set aside.

Combine mayonnaise, momiji oroshi and ginger; mix well and set aside. In a large bowl, combine salmon skin, onion, kaiware, mayonnaise mixture and masago; toss well to combine.

To serve, divide silky tofu onto 4 large plates. Top each piece of tofu with Nalo greens. Place salmon skin mixture on top of bed of greens and sprinkle with nori. Serve at once.

Nori Crusted Sashimi Salad

Chef Mark Ellman, Mala: An Ocean Tavern

Yield: 1 serving

Mark Ellman was one of the 12 Hawai'i Regional Cuisine founders—along with Alan Wong, Sam Choy, Roy Yamaguchi and other trailblazing young chefs who organized in 1991 to take on the westernized foods and flavors that had been engrained in Hawai'i's fine-dining establishment. Their focus was on locally grown produce, to which they applied fine culinary techniques. This salad is a prime example of the approach.

4 ounces 'ahi eye (center cut of loin)
2 tablespoons macadamia nut oil
½ cup furikake
4 slices tomato
3 tablespoons rice vinegar
1 teaspoon fresh ginger, chopped
2 tablespoons chopped fresh mint leaves
1 tablespoon soy sauce
4 cups Kula or Island greens
4 slices avocado
2 tablespoons thinly sliced Maui onion

Roll 'ahi in macadamia nut oil then in furikake. Sear for 5 seconds on each side over very high heat, set aside. Marinate tomatoes in rice vinegar, ginger, mint and soy sauce mixture. Toss greens in the extra marinade of the tomatoes, place in center of plate. Fan avocado to one side of plate, place onions and tomatoes on other side of plate. Slice 'ahi in ¼-inch pieces and arrange around plate.

Pancit Bihon

Chef Almar Arcano

Yield: 6 servings

ancit lends itsself to improvisation, to a jam session at the stovetop where the individual cook can make a mark on the main dish. Like fried rice, this Filipino staple can be simple or complex, full of meat or meatless, the way Mom made it or something very, very different. Pancit simply means noodles. So taken literally, it's any dish made with any type of noodle, although a few central ingredients are generally accepted: bean sprouts, green beans, sliced cabbage, carrots, and patis (fish sauce). This version is from chef Almar Arcano, a personal favorite.

½ cup vegetable oil
1 pound boneless, skinless chicken thighs, sliced
1 tablespoon minced garlic
½ cup each: thinly sliced onion, red and green bell pepper, and carrots
¾ cup each: thinly sliced celery and fresh shiitake mushrooms
1 pound cabbage, sliced
2 cups chicken broth
8 ounces cooked bay shrimps
4 ounces dry squid, cooked and thinly sliced
2 pounds pancit miki (fresh egg noodles)
4 ounces pancit bihon (rice noodles), soaked in water to soften
Achiote powder, soaked in water, as needed
¼ cup oyster sauce
2 tablespoons patis (fish sauce)
1 tablespoon instant soup base
Ground white pepper, to taste

Garnishes:

Cilantro, chopped
Hard-boiled eggs, cut into quarters
Green onion, chopped
Calamansi or lime wedges

Heat oil in a wok. Add chicken, stirring constantly, then the garlic and onion, followed by all the vegetables. Toss to mix and sauté. Pour in broth, then shrimps and squid. Add noodles. Keep tossing mixture. Stir in achiote, oyster sauce, patis, and soup base. If mixture is too dry, add more broth. Season with pepper and garnish.

Fried Rice

Yield: 4 to 6 servings

Does anyone really need a recipe for fried rice? Isn't the dish by nature a hodge-podge of whatever's in the fridge? Of course, but a few rules do seem to apply when this Chinese dish is served on local tables. No. 1, the meat; although you can fancy it up with shrimp or chicken, what's essential is something fatty and salty—Spam®, bacon, char sui, or all three. A bit of egg and green onions is desired. For flavoring, something salty (oyster sauce, soy sauce or dashi-no-moto). The rice should be leftover, dried out in the refrigerator at least overnight. This provides the right texture (not too chewy). As for vegetables? Whatever's in the fridge. And if you don't have any, the green onions will provide appropriate color.
—MURIEL MIURA

½ cup diced meat (char siu, ham, Portuguese sausage, luncheon
    meat or shrimp)
2 slices bacon, chopped
3 tablespoons vegetable oil
4 cups cold cooked rice, preferably day old
⅓ cup chopped green onions
⅓ cup frozen peas and carrots, cooked
⅓ cup oyster sauce
1 teaspoon salt
1 tablespoon dashi-no-moto (fish broth granules)
1 egg, beaten

Stir-fry meat and bacon in hot oil 30 seconds; add rice and stir-fry additional minute. Add green onion, peas and carrots, oyster sauce, salt, and dashi-no-moto; mix well. Add egg and cook 30 seconds, stirring well.

Chinese Steamed Buns or Mantou

Yield: 32 mantou

These elegant buns are the perfect companion to fatty or spicy Chinese dishes. Breads and noodles made with wheat flour, such as the mantou, are typical of northern Chinese cooking, whereas southern Chinese recipes make more use of rice.

Be sure to use all-purpose flour, or even a mixture of all-purpose and cake flour, rather than bread flour. Bread flour has a high gluten content. Low-gluten flour is better for mantou. —AUDREY WILSON

1 teaspoon active dry yeast
⅔ cup warm (100°F) water
1 teaspoon vegetable shortening (to grease a bowl)
3½ cups white all-purpose flour
1 tablespoon + 1 teaspoon sugar
3 teaspoons baking powder
2 tablespoons vegetable shortening (for the dough)
⅔ cup lukewarm milk

Dissolve the yeast in the warm water, and set it aside until foamy, or approximately 5 minutes.

Grease another bowl with 1 teaspoon shortening, set aside.

Sift the flour, sugar, and baking powder together. Using your fingers, work in 2 tablespoons shortening until the mixture resembles coarse meal. Add this flour mixture to the yeast mixture. Add the warm milk and stir the dough until it is stiff.

Turn the dough onto a floured board and knead until smooth, or about 15 minutes. Shape the dough into a ball and transfer it to the oiled bowl; cover the oiled bowl with plastic wrap. Set the dough aside in a warm place until it has doubled in size, or about 2 hours.

Grease the slats of bamboo steamer with oil so that the dough does not stick. Divide the mantou dough into 32 balls and flatten them into 3-inch diameter disks. Brush the surface of the disks with canola oil, then fold the disks in half to form half-moon shaped buns. Let the shaped buns rest in the steamer basket for 15 minutes.

Steam the buns until they are light and puffy, or about 15 minutes. You can serve the buns with Chinese parsley sprigs, green onion strips, Chinese plum sauce, and mango chutney.

Sweet Kula Corn Pudding

❧ Yield: 6 servings ❧

Fresh corn is good, but the sugar starts to break down soon after it is harvested. Refrigeration slows down the process. Corn is high in fiber and carbohydrates, and low in sodium. The farmers deliver Maui Super Sweet Corn from Kula daily.

Emeril Lagasse presented a classic Southern-style corn pudding. My recipe uses fresh, plump Kula corn. We stepped up the presentation by lining the muffin tins with the corn husks to create a mini cupcake serving. This recipe is understated! Try it and you'll understand.
—TYLUN PANG

6 ears fresh Kula sweet corn (or the freshest corn you can buy)
2 tablespoons finely diced Kula onions (or local sweet onions)
½ cup grated Parmesan cheese
2 tablespoons butter
2 cups heavy cream
1 cup milk
6 whole eggs
½ cup corn meal
1 teaspoon salt
¼ teaspoon white pepper
⅛ teaspoon nutmeg

Preheat the oven to 350°F.

Shuck the corn, saving the husks. Using a coarse grater, grate the corn kernels off the cob and into a bowl. Dice the onions. Grate the Parmesan cheese if you aren't using commercial pre-grated cheese.

Heat the butter in a frying pan over medium heat. Sauté the onions in the butter until they have softened; add the grated corn and continue to sauté on moderate heat for another 3 minutes.

Put the cream, milk, eggs, and cheese in a mixing bowl and whisk together. Add this to the corn mixture, stirring constantly over low heat. Gradually add the corn meal, salt, pepper, and nutmeg, and continue cooking and stirring for another 1½ minutes.

Spray a 6-cup muffin tin with non-stick spray and line the cups with the saved corn husks. The husks make natural muffin cups. Divide the batter evenly between the cups. Bake at 350°F for approximately 20 minutes or until the tops are nicely browned and the centers of the muffins are no longer liquid. (Use a toothpick or paring knife to test.)

Cabbage Kim Chee

Dong Yang Inn

Yield: About 1 quart

Kim chee is central to Korean cuisine, eaten at breakfast, dinner and lunch, and appreciated in varying styles, heat levels and with various vegetables as the base. The difference between real Korean kim chee and what you can buy from most local supermarkets is a matter of flavor and fizz. Korean kim chee is much hotter, with more anchovies and patis in a thicker sauce. It's also fermented longer, so it has a tart, spritzy taste. Our version is milder, normally made with Chinese cabbage, and is eaten after a couple days of fermentation which gives it a more fresh and crisp taste.

2 pounds won bok (Chinese cabbage, napa)
½ cup rock salt
4 cups water

Seasonings:

2 teaspoons minced red pepper
¼ teaspoon minced garlic
½ teaspoon minced fresh ginger
½ teaspoon paprika
1 tablespoon sugar

Wash won bok and cut in 1½ inch lengths. Dissolve rock salt in water. Soak won bok in brine 3 to 4 hours; rinse and drain. Combine seasonings and add to won bok, mixing thoroughly. Pack into 1-quart jar. Cover loosely and let stand at room temperature 1 to 2 days. Chill in refrigerator before serving.

Cucumber Kim Chee

Dong Yang Inn

Yield: About 4 pounds

4 pounds cucumber (Japanese variety preferred)
2 tablespoons salt
1 teaspoon fish sauce
1 teaspoon juice from salted baby shrimp (see note)
1 teaspoon minced garlic
½ teaspoon minced ginger
2 tablespoons sugar
1 tablespoon chili pepper powder or ground fresh chili pepper

Quarter cucumber lengthwise and cut into 1½ inch lengths. Mix with salt and let sit 30 minutes. Rinse and drain. Combine with remaining ingredients, mixing by hand (use plastic gloves). May be served immediately.

Note: *Salted baby shrimp is sold in bottles at Korean markets such as Palama Supermarket or Asian markets. To extract juice, squeeze a handful of shrimp.*

Sweet Kula Onion Soup

Yield: 6 servings

Sweet Kula onions are the key ingredients to this delightful onion soup. The onions for this recipe come from Bryan Otani Farms in Upcountry Kula. If you have a chance to visit this wonderful family-run operation, you will find more than just onions. They have string beans, eggplant, red cabbage, and much more, depending on the season. Their sustainably grown produce can be found in select Maui markets.

> 4 pounds sweet Kula onions
> 4 tablespoons butter
> 1 teaspoon salt
> ½ cup dry sherry
> 4 cups beef broth
> 4 cups chicken broth
> 4 fresh sprigs of thyme
> 1 bay leaf
> 12 slices (½-inch thick) from a long French baguette
> 6 (1-ounce) slices Gruyère cheese

Peel and slice the onions; slices should be approximately ¼-inch thick.

Heat the butter in a heavy-bottomed, 2-gallon soup pot set over medium heat. Add the onions and salt and sauté until the onions are soft and nicely caramelized. This will take at least 30 minutes; keep the heat moderate and stir periodically to keep the onions from burning. Don't rush this process.

Deglaze the pot with the sherry, and add the chicken and beef stock. Bring to a boil. Add the thyme and bay leaf (if you're going to remove them later, add them in a spice bag). Turn heat down and simmer on low for 30 minutes. Remove the herbs and season with salt and pepper.

Toast the sliced baguettes.

Preheat the oven to 400°F.

Divide the onion soup between 6 oven-proof soup bowls. Top each bowl with two slices of toasted baguette and a slice of Gruyère cheese. Bake in a 400°F oven until the cheese is browned, or about 5 minutes. Check the soup occasionally to make sure that you don't burn the cheese.

Oxtail Soup

Side Street Inn

Yield: 20 servings

Oxtail soups and stews are found in many cultures, dating to times when no part of an animal was wasted. The version we consider "local" is very Asian, with ginger and star anise common to the seasonings. This version, which has both Chinese and Japanese influences, is served at Side Street Inn once a week as a lunch-time special and it's usually gone by noon, owner Colin Nishida says. His patrons swear by it as a hangover remedy. The Side Street kitchen operates without written recipes, so this formula is an approximation, based on Nishida's notes taken during the making of one batch. Don't expect it to come out exactly the same as the restaurant's.

10 to 15 pounds oxtails, washed and cut in 1 ½ inch pieces, fat-trimmed
1 cup peeled, sliced, smashed ginger
4 cloves garlic, peeled and smashed
12 dried Chinese dates
6 pieces star anise
½ onion
1 stalk celery
1 carrot, peeled
6 tablespoons salt
1 tablespoon pepper
1 cup sake (rice wine)
4 pieces konnyaku (tuber root flour cake), cubed

Garnishes:

10 shiitake mushrooms, soaked, stemmed and halved
1 bunch mustard cabbage, cut in pieces and blanched
1 bunch cilantro, chopped

Cover oxtails in water and boil 15 minutes. Discard water and wash oxtails again to remove blood and smell. Return oxtails to pot and cover with 3 times as much water. Bring to a boil and skim impurities. Add ginger, garlic, dates, star anise, onion, celery and carrot. (Halve onion; put celery and carrot in whole.) Keep at a soft boil for 2 hours, skimming often, until oxtails begin to soften. The meat should not be falling off the bone. Remove dates, carrot, celery, star anise and ginger. Add salt and pepper, sake and konyaku; taste and add more salt and pepper if needed. Simmer 5 minutes.

Garnish each bowl of soup with mushrooms, mustard cabbage and cilantro. Delicious served with steamed rice, grated ginger and soy sauce.

Note: *Nishida says his restaurant does not put peanuts in the soup, but if you believe they're necessary, throw in a handful with the other garnishes.*

Portuguese Bean Soup

Larry Rocha

Yield: 8 to 10 servings

Larry Rocha is known for his "GPS," or Good Portuguese Soup. He dishes up big bowls of GPS at the Maui County Fair's Maui Veterans booth. It's a great soup; you can taste the aloha in every spoonful. He was kind enough to share his recipe.

    3 quarts water
    2 packages (16-ounce) dried red kidney beans, washed
    2 ham hocks
    2 (12-ounce) Portuguese sausages (Ah Fook brand preferred)
    1 medium-sized round onion, roughly chopped
    3 cans (5-ounce) tomato sauce
    3 medium-sized potatoes, peeled and cut into 1-inch dice
    4 medium-sized carrots, peeled and cut into 1-inch dice
    1 bunch (16-ounce) watercress, cut into 3-inch lengths
    Soy sauce to taste (Aloha brand preferred)
    Salt and pepper to taste

Fill a large soup pot with 3 quarts of water and start it heating over medium-high heat. Rinse the kidney beans and chop the Portuguese sausage and the onion per the instructions in the ingredients list. Add the ham hock, Portuguese sausage, kidney beans, chopped onion, and tomato sauce to the pot. Bring the soup to a boil, then turn the heat down and simmer the soup on low for 1½ hours, or until the ham falls off the hock bones. Stir occasionally, and add extra water as needed to keep the soup from burning.

While the soup is cooking, cut up the potatoes, carrots, and watercress per the ingredients list.

Remove the sausage and ham hock from the soup. Cut the meat off the ham hocks and chop it into small pieces, discarding the rest of the hock. Set the sausage and ham chunks aside.

Add the chopped potatoes and carrots to the soup and simmer them until they are tender, about 20 minutes. Put the cut-up sausage and ham back into the soup, together with the cut-up watercress. Turn off the heat under the pot. Taste the soup; add a dash of soy sauce and taste again. Correct the seasoning if necessary.

Traditionally served with one scoop rice.

{ SALADS, SOUPS, AND SIDES }

The Japanese custom of gift-giving, omiyage, is a way of showing appreciation for loved ones while away traveling. This adopted tradition has been widely embraced and adopted by the people of Hawai'i as it fits in well with the Islands' culture of aloha and generosity. It's a way to share Hawai'i with those who couldn't come, as well as a way to bring a little bit of home to loved ones and former residents who are being visited.

All kinds of "only in Hawai'i" treats can be found: sweet and salty bags of crackseed from the corner store, cookies, chips, dried fruits. Perhaps the most welcome and appreciated gift is the one that's homemade. Why purchase a box of goodies when you can make some using the Island's many unique ingredients? From edamame to Hawaiian salt to tropical fruits, the list of available ingredients await for you to make the perfect temiyage (casual, small gift).

OMIYAGE

Crispy Coconut Cookies

Yield: About 4 dozen

Cookies make great gifts and tend to ship well. Crispy cookies, however, need to be packed very well to avoid crumbling. These cookies also make great hostess gifts. —Muriel Miura

- 1 cup butter or margarine
- 1 cup sugar
- 1½ teaspoons vanilla extract
- 2 cups flour
- 1½ cups shredded coconut

In large mixing bowl, cream butter and sugar until light and fluffy. Add vanilla extract; beat thoroughly. Mix in flour; add coconut and mix well. Shape into walnut-size balls and place on ungreased baking sheets; flatten with bottom of a glass dipped in flour. Bake at 300°F for 20 to 25 minutes or until golden brown. Cool completely and store in airtight container at room temperature.

∽ Variations:

Crispy Chocolate Chip: Add 1 cup chocolate chip morsels to dough; omit shredded coconut.

Crispy Hazelnut: Add ¾ cup chopped hazelnuts after flour has been added; omit shredded coconut.

Crispy Lemon: Add 2 tablespoons lemon zest after the flour has been added; omit shredded coconut.

Crispy Macadamia Nut: Add ½ cup macadamia nut bits after flour has been added; omit shredded coconut.

Crispy Spicy: Blend together 1½ teaspoons ground cinnamon, ½ teaspoon ground ginger and ¼ teaspoon nutmeg and add to mixture after flour has been added.

Spicy Seasoned Hawaiian Salt

Yield: About 8 cups

Simply "basic" best describes the flavors this seasoned salt imparts on steaks, chops, roasts, stews, soups and generally everything! Back to basics is a good thing!—MURIEL MIURA

5 pounds Hawaiian salt
⅓ cup coarse black pepper
⅓ cup minced garlic
⅓ cup grated fresh ginger
Crushed chili pepper to taste

Combine salt and pepper in large roasting pan; mix well. Add garlic and ginger using back of wooden spoon to mix well and mash pieces. Bake at 350°F for 25 to 30 minutes, stirring every 2 to 3 minutes, or until slightly brown and dry. Cool thoroughly. Store in covered jar in a cool place.

Use: Great on broiled or baked meats, fish, seafood and poultry. It is often used to flavor soups and stews.

Hawaiian Nut Bread

Yield: One 9 x 5 loaf

Pineapple flourished in Hawai'i during the 20th century. Its exotic, sweet flavor and versatility for cooking delighted chefs and homemakers alike. It has become a widely-used ingredient in Island cooking. In this dish, the pineapple is complemented by the banana flavor. This quick bread can be served at breakfast or for dessert. —MURIEL MIURA

- 2 cups flour
- 2 teaspoons baking powder
- 1 teaspoon baking soda
- ½ teaspoon salt
- 1 can (8¼ oz.) crushed pineapple, including liquid
- 1 cup mashed bananas
- ¼ cup orange juice
- ½ cup butter
- ¾ cup sugar
- 2 eggs
- 2 cups macadamia nut bits

Grease or spray 9 x 5 x 3-inch loaf pan. Sift flour with baking powder, baking soda and salt. In separate bowl, combine pineapple, including liquid, bananas and orange juice. In large mixing bowl, cream butter and sugar until light and fluffy; add eggs, one at a time, beating well after each addition. Add flour mixture alternately with pineapple mixture, mixing only enough to moisten dry ingredients. Stir in nuts. Pour into prepared pan. Bake at 350°F for 60 to 75 minutes or until done.

Dried Cranberry-Edamame Trail Mix

Yield: 10 bags (7 oz. each)

A wonderful, healthy, and delicious snack, this dish is made with dried, sweetened cranberries which are low cholesterol, fat free and a good source of fiber. Combined with dry-roasted edamame, this recipe is a great source of soy protein as well. Enjoy!—MURIEL MIURA

1 package (48 oz.) dried cranberries
1 container (29 oz.) dry roasted edamame (soy beans)

Combine dried cranberries and edamame in a large bowl; toss to mix well. Pack seven ounces of mix in zip-top plastic bags, sealable cellophane bags or clean jars with covers. Seal and store in cool place.

Dried Fruit Mui

Yield: 1 gallon

During the Second World War "cracked seed" (preserved plum) was unavailable due to rationing. Island moms got creative by substituting the plum with other fruits. In my neighborhood as a girl, prune mui was popular because the fruit was easily found at the market. —MURIEL MIURA

1 pound dark brown sugar
3 tablespoons Hawaiian salt
3 tablespoons whiskey
1 tablespoon Chinese five-spice powder
2 cups fresh lemon juice
8 packages (12 oz. each) pitted prunes
2 packages (12 oz. each) dried apricots or mixed dried fruit
½ pound Chinese dried lemon peel, chopped
½ pound seedless li hing mui (dried plum)

In gallon-size plastic jar with lid, combine brown sugar, salt, whiskey, Chinese five-spice powder and lemon juice; mix well to combine. Add prunes and other dried fruits, lemon peel and li hing mui; cover and shake jar to coat fruits. Let stand for a minimum of 3 days at room temperature, mixing twice a day. Pack in plastic containers.

Char Siu Rub

Yield: About 25 cups

Char siu is a popular type of flavoring used for many Chinese roasts. Islanders will be most familiar with it as the sweet barbecued roast pork served as a side dish or garnish in many local favorites. Below, Chef Tylun Pang of Maui shares his recipe for Char Siu Rub. This rub can be bottled and given as an omiyage or used to prepare delicious char siu flavored meats.

    5 pounds sugar
    ¾ cups salt
    2 tablespoons white pepper
    2 tablespoons Chinese five-spice powder*
    ¼ cup fermented red bean curd (nam yui)* with the liquid
    ¼ cup hoisin sauce*
    Few drops red food color, optional
    Honey to glaze

Combine the fermented red bean curd and hoisin sauce in a large bowl; mix well. Gradually add all the sugar and continue to mix. This will help break down any lumps from the bean curd. Next mix in the white pepper, Chinese five spice powder and the red food color. Continue mixing until all ingredients are incorporated. Store in covered jars in a cool place until ready to use. A pound of this rub should be enough to marinate approximately 5 pounds of meat.

When ready to use, rub the mix generously using disposable gloves onto the meat covering all surfaces well and place the seasoned meat into a sealed bag. Juices from the meat will create a sauce let this marinate for 3 days turning periodically. Meat will be ready to cook on day 3.

When ready to cook, remove meat out of the marinade and place on rack in foil-lined pan to catch the drippings. This will make clean-up easier and not ruin your pan with burnt sugar drippings. Bake at 450°F for 20 minutes. Turn heat down to 350°F. and continue to cook until meat is done (use meat thermometer). Cooking time will depend on the meat selected and size of meat. Brush the meat with honey and serve.

Suggested Meats: Pork loin, strips of pork butt, baby back ribs, country style ribs, chicken thighs or my favorite turkey tails.

* Chinese ingredients may be found at Asian grocery stores or in the oriental section of most supermarkets.

'Ulu Chips

Yield: 6 servings

When breadfruit is ripe it's sweet and fruity. Half-ripe 'ulu is still starchy and firm; this is the best kind to use for chips.

If you have a deep fryer that maintains an even temperature, these chips will be easy. If you are frying in a wok, a big pot, or a deep Dutch oven, be sure to use a deep-frying thermometer to ensure that the oil stays at the proper temperature. That's the key to successful deep-frying. —AUDREY WILSON

1 half-ripe 'ulu (breadfruit)
Oil for deep-frying
Garlic salt

Wash the half-ripe 'ulu. Cut off the stem, then cut the 'ulu in half lengthwise. No need to peel. Slice the 'ulu halves, as thinly as possible. It's hard to get them thin enough with a knife. A cook's mandoline would be extremely helpful here.

Cover the bottom of a baking pan or cookie sheet with paper towels. Heat the deep-frying oil to 350°F.

Slide a few 'ulu chips at a time into the heated oil and fry. The chips will turn light brown when they are done; this should take about 3 minutes.

Put the cooked chips into the towel-lined pan and sprinkle them with garlic salt. To remove any grease left over from the deep-frying, you can leave the chips on the towels until the towels have soaked up the grease. You might also try putting the cooked chips in a salad spinner and spinning them to remove the oil.

Years ago, Hawaiian desserts came in two flavors: pineapple and coconut. Today's island favorite desserts reflect the full range of island influences, from the haupia of old Hawai'i to the mochi of Japan. Some may not seem all that "local," but often when people move away from Hawai'i, they often can no longer find the sweets they used to take for granted. What makes this selection "local" is its pure variety with influences from the many ethnic groups that contribute to our mixed plate, sometimes blended with ideas borrowed from other areas.

A good dessert is the ultimate goal of any meal, the sweet ending everyone at the table is working towards. This is a treasury of desserts that has been pleasing people in Hawai'i for decades. Each one tastes scrumptious.

DESSERTS

Red Velvet Cake

This cake and its surreal coloring has roots in the American South and dates back generations, but it's undergoing a resurgence in upscale bakeries across the country. In Hawai'i, though, the cake never lost its place at the potluck table. The cake is a cousin of Devil's Food Cake, with the red coloring being a reaction of the cocoa to the acid in the buttermilk. But most cooks accentuate the coloring with a hefty pour of food coloring. —MURIEL MIURA

1 cup butter or margarine
1½ cups sugar
2 eggs
½ teaspoon salt
2 tablespoons cocoa powder

2½ cups cake flour
1¼ teaspoons baking soda
1 cup buttermilk
1½ bottles (1 oz. size) red food coloring

Cream butter and sugar until light and fluffy. Add eggs, one at a time, beating well after each addition. Sift dry ingredients together. Add to butter mixture alternately with buttermilk, beginning and ending with flour mixture. Pour batter into two lightly greased and floured 8 or 9-inch layer pans. Bake at 350°F for 30 to 35 minutes or until done. Cool and frost with Butter Cream Frosting (recipe follows).

Tip: Most cakes freeze well for 4 to 6 months. Thaw without unwrapping or removing from the frozen container.

Butter Cream Frosting

Yield: About 2½ cups

⅓ cup butter or margarine, softened
4 cups confectioners' sugar, sifted
1½ teaspoons vanilla extract
2 to 3 tablespoons evaporated milk

Cream butter and half the sugar, blending well. Add vanilla and gradually blend in remaining sugar. Add enough milk until of desired spreading consistency. Frost an 8- or 9-inch layer cake.

Lava Cake

Yield: 6 servings

A chocolate cake by itself is a treat, but a chocolate cake with a soft chocolate center is decadence personified! What's more, this dessert is simple and easy to prepare. The batter can be prepared the day before, refrigerated and baked just before serving. —MURIEL MIURA

1 package (6 squares) bittersweet baking chocolate (Valrohna, Scharffen Berger preferred), break into pieces
¼ pound (½ cup) butter, cut into chunks
1½ cups confectioner's sugar
½ cup flour
3 whole eggs
3 egg yolks

Suggested Garnishes:
Sweetened whipped cream
Ice cream
6 fresh raspberries

Grease six 6-ounce ovenproof custard cups, ramekins or soufflé dishes. Place on baking sheet; set aside.

Microwave chocolate and butter in large microwaveable bowl on HIGH 1 minute or MEDIUM (50%) 2 minutes or until butter is melted. Stir with wire whisk until chocolate is completely melted. Add sugar and flour; mix well. Whisk in whole eggs and egg yolks; beat until well blended. Divide batter evenly into prepared ovenproof dishes. Bake at 425°F for 10 to 14 minutes, or until cakes are firm around the edges but still soft in the centers. Let stand 1 minute. Run small knife around cakes to loosen. Invert cakes carefully onto dessert dishes. To serve, cut in half, if desired; garnish with additional confectioner's sugar lightly sprinkled on top, dollop of sweetened whipped cream or ice cream and top with fresh raspberries. Serve warm.

Flavor variations: Prepare as directed. Add 1 teaspoon pure almond extract, orange extract, vanilla extract, raspberry extract or ground cinnamon to batter. If desired, prepare batter day before and pour into prepared cups or dishes; cover with plastic wrap; refrigerate. Bring to room temperature when ready to serve, uncover and bake as directed.

Pineapple Upside Down Cake

Yield: About 20 to 24 servings

Upside-down cakes date to a time before reliable ovens, when cakes were often cooked on the stovetop, usually in a cast-iron skillet. Butter and sugar were caramelized in the bottom of the skillet, and the batter went on top. When the cake was inverted—voila! a cake with a golden glaze on top. Fruits and nuts were normally part of the glaze. Hawai'i's part in this comes through the Hawaiian Pineapple Co. (later Dole Foods), which popularized the pineapple version of the cake by publishing the recipe in magazine ads as a way to help sell its Hawaiian pineapple. The pineapple version is the modern standard for upside-down cakes.
—MURIEL MIURA

½ cup butter or margarine
1½ cups brown sugar, packed
1 can (1 pound 4 oz.) sliced pineapple, drained
10 maraschino cherries
1 package (18.5 oz.) yellow cake mix

Melt butter or margarine in 13 x 9 x 2-inch pan. Stir in brown sugar and spread evenly in pan. Arrange pineapple slices on sugar mixture; place cherries in center of pineapple slices.

Prepare cake according to package directions. Pour batter over fruit, spreading evenly. Bake at 350°F oven for 35 to 40 minutes or until golden brown and wooden pick inserted in cake comes our clean. Cool slightly; invert onto a serving platter.

Tip: Serve warm cake slices topped with ice cream, whipped cream, fruit, sour cream, yogurt, or your favorite sauce or pudding.

Coconut Cake

Yield: Two layer 8-inch cake

A slightly different take on the classic coconut cake, this recipe uses coconut not only in the frosting, but also in the batter. This gives the cake a wonderful flaky texture. It's delicious, too. Give it a try!
—MURIEL MIURA

1¾ cups sifted cake flour	2 eggs
2¼ teaspoons baking powder	⅔ cup milk
¾ teaspoon salt	1 teaspoon vanilla
½ cup butter or margarine	⅔ cup Angel Flake coconut
1 cup + 2 tablespoons sugar	

Measure sifted flour, baking powder and salt; sift together. Cream butter and sugar until light and fluffy. Add eggs, one at a time, beating well after each addition. Alternately add flour mixture and milk, beating well after each additional until smooth. Stir in vanilla and coconut. Pour batter into two 8-inch greased and floured layer pans. Bake at 350°F for 30 to 35 minutes or until done. Cool in pans 10 minutes; then remove from pans and finish cooling on racks. Frost with Haupia Frosting (see below) or sweetened whipped cream to serve.

Haupia Frosting

Yield: About 2 cups

Haupia is the coconut pudding often served as dessert at a lū'au. It also makes a delicious frosting or topping for cakes and other desserts.

6 tablespoons cornstarch	1 cup heavy cream
6 tablespoons sugar	3 tablespoons sugar
¾ cup water	1 package (4 oz.) frozen
1 can (12 oz.) frozen coconut milk, thawed	shredded coconut, thawed

Mix cornstarch with sugar and water in saucepan. Stir in coconut milk and cook over low heat, stirring constantly, until mixture thickens. Remove from heat; cool slightly. Spread between layers and on top of cake. Let cool until haupia is firm.

Whip cream until soft peaks form; add sugar slowly and continue beating until stiff peaks form. Spread sweetened whipped cream on top

Pineapple-Carrot Cake

Yield: 2 (9-inch) cakes

Carrot cake gets even better when it's made with fresh local produce. We like to use Hāna organic red carrots and Maui Gold pineapple, a sweet, low-acid pineapple that works beautifully in baked goods. If you can't get the Hāna carrots, use the sweetest, tastiest organic carrots that you can find. It makes a big difference in the flavor.
—TYLUN PANG

- 2 cups finely shredded, organic carrots
- 1 cup Maui Gold pineapple, small diced
- 3 cups all-purpose flour
- 1 tablespoon cinnamon
- 1½ teaspoons baking soda
- ½ teaspoon salt
- 4 large eggs
- 1½ cups organic canola oil
- 2½ cups sugar

Peel and finely shred the carrots. Peel and core the pineapple, if starting with a whole pineapple, and cut the meat into ¼-inch chunks.

Preheat oven to 350°F. Oil and flour two 9-inch cake pans.

Sift together the flour, cinnamon, baking soda, and salt. Beat the 4 eggs; mix the eggs, sugar, and oil. Add about ⅓ of the dry ingredients to the egg-oil mixture and mix well. Repeat until all the dry ingredients have been added. Fold in the grated carrots and cut-up pineapple.

Pour the batter into the oiled and floured pans. Bake in the 350°F oven for about 35 to 40 minutes, or until a toothpick or paring knife inserted in the middle of the cake comes out clean.

Remove the cakes from the pans and cool on a wire rack. You can serve the sliced cake dusted with powdered sugar and freshly whipped cream.

Macadamia Nut Chiffon Cake

Yield: 8 to 10 servings

Chiffon cakes are as light as an angel food cake and have the richness of a butter cake. They're popular among homemakers because they're relatively easy to make. —Muriel Miura

9 egg whites (1¼ cups)
1½ cups sugar
¾ cup flour
1½ teaspoons ground cinnamon
1 teaspoon salt
9 egg yolks
1½ teaspoons vanilla
2 cups macadamia nuts, very finely chopped or ground

Beat egg whites until foamy; gradually beat in ½ cup sugar until stiff and glossy.

Sift together flour, cinnamon and salt. Combine egg yolks, vanilla and remaining sugar; beat until thick and lemon-colored. Stir in dry ingredients. Pour batter into egg whites and fold in gently, but thoroughly. Fold in nuts.

Pour into ungreased 10-inch tube pan. Bake at 350°F for 50 to 60 minutes. Invert to cool. Cool completely before removing from pan. Sprinkle with confectioners' sugar or top with sweetened whipped cream to serve.

Variation: Substitute walnuts for macadamia nuts.

Liliko'i Spice Cake

Yield: 8 to 10 servings

This cake comes from a family of local sweets made with frozen juice concentrate. Fresh liliko'i juice can be hard to come by, but the frozen concentrate can be found in any supermarket. Thawed and undiluted, the concentrate is an easy way to add tropical flavor to cakes, pies, sorbets and mochi. —MURIEL MIURA

3 cups cake flour
1 teaspoon ground cinnamon
1 teaspoon ground cloves
½ teaspoon allspice
2 teaspoons baking powder
1 teaspoon baking soda
1 cup butter or margarine, softened
2 cups sugar
4 egg yolks
½ cup thawed liliko'i (passion fruit) frozen concentrate
½ cup water
4 egg whites

Liliko'i Frosting:

2 egg whites
1 cup sugar
¼ teaspoon salt
⅓ cup thawed liliko'i (passion fruit) concentrate
⅓ cup water

To prepare cake, sift together cake flour, cinnamon, cloves, allspice, baking powder, and baking soda; set aside. Cream butter or margarine together with sugar until light and fluffy. Add egg yolks, one at a time, beating well after each addition. Add flour mixture alternately with liliko'i concentrate and water, beginning and ending with flour.

Beat egg whites until stiff but not dry. Fold batter into the beaten egg whites then pour batter into two 9-inch greased and floured 8 or 9-inch cake pans. Bake at 350°F for 35 to 40 minutes or until cake is done. Set aside to cool.

To prepare Liliko'i Frosting, combine all frosting ingredients in a large saucepan. Beat mixture with hand mixer. Cook over low heat, beating constantly, until frosting forms stiff peaks, about 7 to 10 minutes. Makes about 2½ cups. Frost cooled layer cake.

Guava Chiffon Pie

Yield: 8 servings

The common guava found in Hawai'i has a unique flowery-fruity flavor and makes a perfect ingredient for desserts. Fresh fruits are rarely available for picking from the roadsides today, but the fruit juice is widely available in markets in cans—either chilled, room temperature, or frozen. —MURIEL MIURA

1 envelope unflavored gelatin
¼ cup cold water
4 eggs, separated
¼ cup lemon juice
3 tablespoons sugar
1 teaspoon lemon zest
1 can (6 oz.) frozen guava juice, thawed
Few drops red food coloring
¼ teaspoon salt
⅓ cup sugar
9-inch baked pie shell
Sweetened whipped cream

Soften gelatin in water. Beat egg yolks well. Combine in saucepan egg yolks, lemon juice and the 3 tablespoons sugar. Cook over low heat, stirring constantly, until mixture thickens. Stir in softened gelatin until gelatin is dissolved. Cool slightly; stir in lemon zest, guava juice and food coloring. Refrigerate and chill until mixture begins to congeal slightly. In small bowl, beat egg whites with salt until soft peaks form; gradually beat in the remaining ⅓ cup sugar. Fold in stiffly beaten egg whites into guava mixture. Pour into baked pie shell; chill until firm. Serve with sweetened whipped cream.

Custard Pie ala Hawai'i

Yield: 1 (9-inch) pie

Due to shortages of fresh milk during the Second World War, Hawai'i bakers began to substitue evaporated milk in their recipes. The taste caught on in Island homes. If you're looking to give your custard desserts a distinctive local flavor, I recommend the use of evaporated milk. —Muriel Miura

5 eggs, slightly beaten
¾ cup sugar
½ teaspoon salt
¼ teaspoon nutmeg
3 cups undiluted evaporated milk
1 teaspoon vanilla extract
9-inch unbaked pie shell

Beat eggs slightly; stir in sugar, salt, nutmeg, milk and vanilla extract. Whisk to blend ingredients well. Pour into pie shell. Bake at 425°F for 30 to 40 minutes, or until knife inserted in center of pie comes out clean.

Hawai'i-Style Andagi

Yield: About 4 dozen

Hot out of the oil, these Okinawan doughnuts are one of the world's great treats. At the annual Okinawan Festival in Kapi'olani Park, tens of thousands of andagi are sold in grease-spotted bags. This version, adapted from Hui O Laulima, the women's auxiliary of the United Okinawan Association of Hawai'i, lightens up the traditional andagi recipe with the addition of milk and vanilla. Skilled andagi makers squeeze the dough out of their fists into perfect balls. It's not that hard, but for your first time you might want to use an ice-cream scoop.

4 cups flour
4 teaspoons baking powder
2 cups sugar
½ teaspoon salt
⅓ cup evaporated milk
2 tablespoons vegetable oil
1 teaspoon vanilla
4 large eggs, slightly beaten
Vegetable oil, for deep frying

Combine flour, baking powder, sugar, and salt. Make a well in center.

Combine milk, oil, and vanilla in a measuring cup, then add enough water to make 1 cup of liquid. Add eggs. Pour into well in dry ingredients. Mix by hand until barely moist. Preheat oil to 350°F. Drop dough by hand, or use a large spoon or ice cream scoop. Fry until golden, about 8 minutes. Andagi is done when a skewer poked into the center comes out clean. Drain on paper towels.

Mango Bread

Yield: 1 (9 x 3-inch) loaf

Wishing for a bumper crop of mangoes this season to bake my favorite Mango Bread … it is quick to make and is more like a cake than bread. It is delicious for breakfast, as a snack or for a casual dessert. It's also a perfect homemade gift plus it freezes well. —MURIEL MIURA

2 cups flour
2 teaspoons baking soda
2 teaspoons ground cinnamon
1¼ cups sugar
½ cup shredded coconut
½ cup chopped nuts (macadamia, walnuts, pecans)
2 cups chopped ripe mangoes
¾ cup canola oil
3 eggs, beaten
2 teaspoons vanilla

Combine flour, baking soda and cinnamon in a mixing bowl; stir in sugar, coconut and nuts. Add remaining ingredients and mix well. Pour into greased and floured 9 x 5 x 3-inch loaf pan. Bake in 350°F oven for 1 hour or until wooden pick inserted in center comes out clean.

{ DESSERTS }

Malassadas

(Portuguese Doughnut)

Yield: About 7 dozen

Leonard's Bakery brought the malassada to Hawai'i on Shrove Tuesday in 1953 (Shrove Tuesday is the day before Lent and for many Catholics is a day of indulgence before the self-deprivation that leads up to Easter). Mary Rego, mother of the bakery's founder, Frank Leonard Rego, suggested trying the traditional treat from her homeland of Portugal. The malassada (that's the Portuguese spelling, although Leonard's has always spelled it with a single S) remains the Kapahulu bakery's No. 1 seller, and the Leonard's malassada trucks are a fixture all over the island. Leonard's recipe is a secret, but here's a basic version.

1 package active dry yeast
1 teaspoon sugar
¼ cup lukewarm water
6 cups flour
½ teaspoon salt
½ cup sugar
6 eggs, beaten until thick
½ teaspoon lemon extract, optional
¼ cup butter or margarine, melted
1 cup evaporated milk, undiluted
1 cup water
1 quart canola oil for deep frying

Sugar
Ground cinnamon, optional

Dissolve yeast and 1 teaspoon sugar in lukewarm water; set aside. Combine flour, salt and sugar in a large mixing bowl; make a well in the center of dry ingredients. Combine yeast mixture with eggs, lemon extract, butter or margarine, milk, and water; mix thoroughly then add to dry mixture. Beat to form soft, smooth dough. Cover; let rise until doubled. Drop dough by generous teaspoonfuls into oil heated to 375°F and fry until both sides are golden brown. Drain on absorbent paper; shake in bag with sugar or sugar-cinnamon mixture and serve immediately.

Coconut Washboards

Yield: About 20 cookies

A popular cookie in the 1920s and 1930s and still popular today in some areas of the country, "washboards" got their name from the ridges made by pressing a fork into the dough before baking. —MURIEL MIURA

½ cup unsalted butter, softened
1 cup light brown sugar, firmly packed
1 teaspoon vanilla
¼ teaspoon coconut extract
1 large whole egg
1 large egg yolk
2 cups unbleached flour
¾ teaspoon double-acting baking powder
¼ teaspoon baking soda
Pinch of salt
1 cup sweetened coconut flakes, packed

In a bowl cream together butter and brown sugar until light; beat in vanilla, coconut extract, whole egg, and egg yolk. In another bowl, sift together flour, baking powder, baking soda, and salt. Stir the flour mixture into the butter mixture; stir in the coconut; cover and chill the dough for 20 minutes or until firm.

Spoon slightly rounded tablespoons of dough into floured palm of hand and form into 2½ inch long logs. Place logs 3 inches apart on greased baking sheets. Using a fork dipped in flour, press the back of the tines lengthwise into the logs, flattening them to 4 inches long and 1½ inches wide. (The marks from the tines of the fork should all be lengthwise.) Bake at 375°F for 10 to 12 minutes or until they are golden around the edges. Cool on baking sheets for 5 minutes then transfer the cookies to racks and cool completely.

Haupia

(Coconut Pudding)

Yield: 16 pieces

Be grateful you don't have to make haupia the old way, using Polynesian arrowroot that had to be grated, soaked, strained, reduced to a paste, and dried, then pounded into a powder. A lot of work for a coconut pudding. These days we have cornstarch, which makes everything easier.
—MURIEL MIURA

⅓ cup sugar
⅓ cup cornstarch
⅛ teaspoon salt
2½ cups coconut milk

Combine sugar, cornstarch and salt; stir in coconut milk. Cook over low heat, stirring constantly, until thickened. Pour into an 8-inch square pan; let cool; refrigerate until firm. Cut into 2 x 2-inch pieces and serve on ti leaves, if desired.

Chi Chi Dango

(Milk Flavored Rice Dumplings)

Yield: About 4 dozen

This treat is so easy to find in Hawai'i that many kids go through culture shock when they move to the mainland and find they can't buy it at Long's anymore. Sweet, sticky Chi Chi Dango is mochi for beginners, with no filling. A few drops of food coloring to turn it pink or green is traditional. —MURIEL MIURA

⅔ cup water
⅔ cup evaporated milk, undiluted
1 (10 oz.) package mochiko (rice flour)

Syrup:
1¼ cups sugar
¼ cup water
Few drops red or green food coloring, optional

Katakuriko (potato starch)

Combine water, milk and mochiko in large bowl; mix well. Wrap in double thickness of wet cheesecloth and steam for 25 to 30 minutes.

Combine sugar and water for syrup and bring to a boil; cool. Pour over steamed mochiko mixture, a little at a time, mixing until well blended. Add coloring, if desired; mix well. Roll in katakuriko then cut into desired size or shape; wrap individually in waxed paper or roll in katakuriko again.

Tip: Kinako (ground toasted soy beans) may be substituted for katakuriko.

Liliko'i Crème Brûlée

Yield: 6 servings

Both liliko'i and passion fruit are known as water lemons. Passion fruit is the sour yellow variety while the purple-skinned liliko'i is sweeter, growing wild in the mountains where its prolific vine bears fruit during summer and fall. Years ago, a liliko'i would be used as a children's pacifier. Smaller than a lemon, it has a rich aroma and flavor. —TYLUN PANG

- **1 cup heavy cream**
- **1 cup milk**
- **½ cup sugar**
- **½ cup pasteurized egg yolks**
- **1 teaspoon vanilla extract**
- **¼ cup liliko'i juice (concentrated)**
- **2 tablespoons sugar**
- **2 tablespoons brown sugar**

In a saucepan bring ½ of the milk and cream mixture to a boil. Take the remaining milk and cream and beat in the egg yolks, then slowly temper all of the hot cream with the cold cream/yolk mixture.

Add vanilla and liliko'i juice at this stage. Pour into 6 small ramekins.

Then bake in a water bath for approx 35 to 40 minutes or until it stops moving.

Remove from oven and cool to room temperature.

Refrigerate for 1 hour, or overnight.

Heat the broiler to high. Mix the 2 tablespoons of sugar and the brown sugar in a small bowl. Sprinkle evenly over the top of the custard. Place the custard about 2 inches from the broiler and broil until the sugar melts; this should take about 2 minutes. Watch the custard carefully, as it will go from melting to burning very quickly.

A home torch would also work.

Remove from heat and allow to cool. Serve.

Weights & Measurements

Teaspoons	Tablespoons	Cups	Ounces	Milliliters/ Liters	Pints/Quarts
¼ tsp				1 ml	
½ tsp				2 ml	
¾ tsp	¼ tbsp			4 ml	
1 tsp	⅓ tbsp			5 ml	
3 tsp	1 tbsp	⅟₁₆ cup	½ oz	15 ml	
6 tsp	2 tbsp	⅛ cup	1 oz	30 ml	
			1½ oz	44 ml	
12 tsp	4 tbsp	¼ cup	2 oz	60 ml	
16 tsp	5⅓ tbsp	⅓ cup	2½ oz	75 ml	
18 tsp	6 tbsp	⅜ cup	3 oz	90 ml	
24 tsp	8 tbsp	½ cup	4 oz	125 ml	¼ pint
32 tsp	10⅔ tbsp	⅔ cup	5 oz	150 ml	
36 tsp	12 tbsp	¾ cup	6 oz	175 ml	
48 tsp	16 tbsp	1 cup	8 oz	237 ml	½ pint
		1½ cups	12 oz	355 ml	
		2 cups	16 oz	473 ml	1 pint
		3 cups	24 oz	710 ml	1½ pints

Substitution of Ingredients

Ingredient	Substitution
1 tablespoon flour *(used as thickener)*	½ tablespoon cornstarch, potato starch, rice starch, or arrowroot starch; or 1 tablespoon quick-cooking tapioca
1 cup sifted all-purpose flour	1 cup unsifted all-purpose flour minus 2 tablespoons
1 cup sifted cake flour	⅞cup sifted all-purpose flour, or 1 cup minus 2 tablespoons sifted all-purpose flour
1 cup corn syrup	1 cup sugar plus ¼ cup liquid*
1 cup honey	1¼ cup sugar plus ¼ cup liquid*
1 ounce chocolate	3 tablespoons cocoa plus 1 tablespoon fat
1 cup butter	1 cup margarine, or ⅞ to 1 cup hydrogenated fat plus ½ teaspoon salt; or ⅞ cup lard plus ½ teaspoon salt
1 cup coffee cream *(20%)*	3 tablespoons butter plus about ⅞ cup milk
1 cup heavy cream *(40%)*	⅓ cup butter plus about ¾ cup milk
1 cup whole milk	1 cup reconstituted nonfat dry milk plus 2½ teaspoons butter or margarine; or ½ cup evaporated milk plus ½ cup water; or ¼ cup sifted dry whole milk powder plus ⅞ cup water
1 cup milk	3 tablespoons sifted regular nonfat dry milk plus 1 cup minus 1 tablespoon water; or ⅓ cup instant nonfat dry milk plus 1 cup minus 1 tablespoon water
1 cup buttermilk or sour milk	1 tablespoon vinegar or lemon juice plus enough sweet milk to make 1 cup (let stand 5 minutes); or 1¾ teaspooons cream of tartar plus 1 cup sweet milk
1 teaspoon baking powder	¼ teaspoon baking soda plus ⅝ teaspoon cream of tartar; or ¼ teaspoon baking soda plus ½ cup fully soured milk or buttermilk; or ¼ teaspoon baking soda plus ½ tablespoon vinegar or lemon juice used with sweet milk to make ½ cup; or ¼ teaspoon baking soda plus ¼ to ½ cup molasses
1 tablespoon active dry yeast	1 package active dry yeast, or 1 compressed yeast cake
1 whole egg	2 egg yolks; or 3 tablespoons plus 1 teaspoon thawed frozen egg; or 2 tablespoons and 2 teaspoons dry whole egg powder plus an equal amount of water
1 egg yolk	3½ teaspoons thawed frozen egg yolk or 2 tablespoons dry egg yolk plus 2 teaspoons water
1 egg white	2 tablespoons thawed frozen egg white; or 2 teaspoons dry egg white plus 2 tablespooons water

* Use whatever liquid is called for in the recipe.

Glossary

{ A }

Achiote powder: Made from the seeds from the lipstick plant, also called annatto or achuete.

Adobo: Filipino seasoned meat, poultry or seafood.

'Ahi: Hawaiian name for yellowfin or bigeye tuna. Served in the Islands as sashimi. Substitute fresh blackfin or bluefin tuna.

Aioli: Garlic mayonnaise.

Aku: The Hawaiian name for skipjack tuna. Deep red in color and stronger tasting than 'ahi. Good broiled, grilled, or used raw in poke. Substitute any tuna.

'Alaea salt: Hawaiian name for a red-tinged sea salt. Iron-rich "red dirt" gives it its color. Substitute sea salt.

Andagi: Okinawan doughnut.

{ B }

Bamboo shoots: Edible shoots of the bamboo plant. Available fresh, dried, and canned.

Bean sprouts: Sprouted mung beans. Consumed raw or lightly stir-fried. Substitute canned mung beans.

Black beans: fermented Chinese black beans used for seasoning; dau see. Substitute other firm beans.

Breadfruit: A bland, starchy vegetable used in the Pacific Islands. Substitute potatoes.

{ C }

Calamari: Another name for SQUID. Substitute octopus.

Char siu: Chinese sweet roasted pork.

Chinese dates: A small red fruit with a pit, available fresh or dried. Commonly called jujube.

Chinese fishcake: Finely ground fish paste.

Chinese five-spice powder: A fragrant, spicy, and slightly sweet spice mixture made from ground star anise, Szechuan peppercorns, fennel seeds, cloves, and cinnamon.

Chinese parsley: See CILANTRO

Chow mein noodles: Chinese soft-fried wheat or egg noodles.

Cilantro: Also called Chinese parsley. The green leaves and stems of the coriander plant. Substitute parsley.

Coconut milk: The rich, creamy liquid extracted by squeezing the grated meat of a coconut. Available fresh, canned, or frozen. Substitute (thin) use: 1 cup whole milk beaten with 1 teaspoon coconut flavoring; (thick) use: 1 cup heavy cream with 1 teaspoon coconut flavoring.

Curry powder: A mixture of spices including cardamom, chili, cinnamon, cloves, coriander, cumin, fennel seeds, fenugreek, mace, nutmeg, red and black pepper, saffron, SESAME SEEDS, tamarind, and turmeric. Different curry powders use different spices in different proportions.

{ D }

Daikon sprouts: See KAIWARE.

Daikon: A large Asian radish, usually white in color used in Japan and Korea for soups and pickles, or eaten raw. Flavors range from mild to spicy-hot. Available fresh, pickled, or preserved. Substitute turnips or radish.

Dashi or dashi-no-moto: A clear, light Japanese fish broth sold as instant stock in granules or tea-like bags, or as a concentrate. Substitute chicken stock.

{ F }

Fish sauce: See PATIS.

Furikake: A Japanese condiment made from dried seaweed flakes, SESAME SEEDS, bonito flakes, sugar, salt, and other seasonings. Substitute ground sesame seeds and finely chopped NORI seaweed sheets.

{ G }

Ginger: The root of the domestic ginger plant. It is used as a seasoning both in savory dishes and in sweets. (Powdered ginger is not a good substitute.)

Guava: A round tropical fruit with a yellow skin and pink inner flesh and many seeds. Grown commercially in Hawai'i. The purée or juice is available as a frozen concentrate. Substitute LILIKO'I.

{ H }

Haupia: Hawaiian coconut pudding.

Hawaiian chili pepper: A small, hot chili pepper grown in Hawai'i. Substitute Thai bird chilies or any small hot chili pepper.

Hawaiian salt: Coarse, heavy, white or red crystals made from evaporated seawater. Substitute kosher salt or sea salt.

Hibachi: A small, portable, inexpensive Japanese outdoor grill.

Hoisin sauce: A thick reddish-brown sauce made with fermented soybeans, garlic, rice, salt, and sugar. Substitute puréed plum baby food mixed with SHOYU, garlic, and chili peppers.

Horseradish: From the mustard family known for its thick, fleshy white roots.

{ I }

Imitation crab: Crab-flavored fish product.

Imu: The old Hawai'i underground earth oven lined with fire-heated stones covered with banana stalks and banana leaves.

'Inamona: Hawaiian word for a relish (in paste or chopped form) made from roasted KUKUI NUTS and salt. Substitute coarsely chopped salted cashew nuts.

{ J }

Juhn: Korean term for meat and vegetables cooked in egg batter

{ K }

Kālua: Hawaiian method of cooking food in an underground pit called an imu. Substitute turkey.

Kaiware: Japanese name for DAIKON radish sprouts. Substitute clover sprouts.

Kalbi: Korean barbecued short ribs.

Kamaboko: A Japanese seafood product used mostly in Japanese soup or noodle dishes; also called fish cake.

Kampachi: Highly-prized Hawaiian yellowtail fish.

Katakuriko: Finely ground potato starch.

Kiawe: Locally found tree whose wood charcoal (mesquite) is excellent for grilling.

Kim chee: A Korean pickled vegetable usually made with Chinese cabbage (WON BOK), vinegar, salt, garlic, and chili peppers. Can be very hot and spicy. Substitute pickled cucumbers or cabbage with garlic and chili peppers.

Kinako: Roasted whole soybean flour that has been finely ground.

Ko choo jung: Korean sauce made from mochi rice and chili peppers. May also contain BLACK BEANS, garlic, and spices. Also spelled kochujang or gochujang. Substitute any chili paste.

Konbu: Dried kelp.

Konnyaku: Japanese yam cake, typically gray or white in color.

Kukui nuts: Hawaiian name for the candlenut. See also 'INAMONA, a relish made with roasted kukui nuts. Substitute roasted cashew nuts.

{ L }

Laulau: Packages of TI LEAVES or banana leaves containing pork, beef, salted fish, or TARO tops. Laulau are baked in an IMU or in a regular gas or electric oven.

Liliko'i: A tangy, plum-sized, multi-seeded tropical fruit. Also known as passion fruit. Sold as frozen concentrate. Substitute frozen concentrate liliko'i or orange juice.

Limu kohu: An edible red seaweed that may range in color from tan through shades of pink to dark red. Hawaiians considered it a great treat. It is generally rolled into balls and dried after it is collected. Substitute kelp.

Lomi: Hawaiian term meaning to crush ingredients with fingers.

Long rice: Translucent thread-like noodles made from mung bean flour. Typically needs to be soaked in water before cooking.

Lū'au leaves: The young green tops of the taro root. Substitute fresh spinach.

Lū'au: Hawaiian name for feast.

Lumpia (wrappers): A thin wheat wrapper filled with minced vegetables, bits of meat, seafood, or TOFU. Served either uncooked or deep-fried.

Lup cheong: Sweetened, dried Chinese sausage.

{ M }

Macadamia nuts: Round, oily nuts with a creamy, slightly crunchy texture, harvested from trees, and grown on the Big Island. Substitute pine nuts.

Mahimahi: Also called dolphinfish, it has a firm, pink flesh. Best fresh but often available frozen. Substitute snapper, catfish, or halibut.

Mango: An oval tropical fruit with golden-orange flesh and an enticing, aromatic flavor; skin color ranges from yellow-orange to burgundy to green. Substitute peaches or sweet ripe nectarines.

Maui onion: A sweet, mild onion, originally grown in the Kula district of Maui.

Mirin: Japanese sweet rice wine. Substitute cream sherry or sweet vermouth.

Misoyaki: Japanese dish; meat or fish marinated in miso then broiled.

Miso: A soybean paste made by salting and fermenting soybeans and rice. Shiro miso, or white miso, is the mildest of several types. Available shrink-wrapped, or in cans and jars. Can be refrigerated for months. Substitute condensed chicken broth blended with a small amount of TOFU.

Mochi: Steamed or pounded rice cake.

Mochiko: Japanese glutinous rice flour used in making pastries and some sauces.

Mushrooms: Most commonly seen mushrooms in Hawai'i are button mushrooms, enoki, oyster mushrooms, portobello mushrooms, and SHIITAKE MUSHROOMS.

{ N }

Namasu: Japanese salad made with pickled carrots, DAIKON, and vinegar marinade.

Nori: Paper-thin sheets of seasoned, dried seaweed used for SUSHI; laver.

{ O }

Ogo: Japanese name for Gracilaria seaweed. Several Hawai'i aquaculture operations grow ogo, and it is widely available. Substitute finely julienned crisp cucumbers plus bits of dried NORI seaweed, or try rinsed sweet or dill pickles.

Okinawan sweet potato: Purple sweet potato.

'Ono: Hawaiian word for delicious.

Ono: Hawaiian word for the fish also known as wahoo.

Opah: Ocean moonfish.

'Ōpakapaka: Local deep-water fish. Its sweet, delicate flesh is always white when cooked. Runs from lean to fat, depending on the season.

Oxtail: Tail of cattle which is sold skinned and cut into short pieces. Usually used for stews, braised, or as a soup stock.

Oyster sauce: A thick brown sauce made from oysters, brine, and SHOYU. Used in many stir-fried dishes. Substitute regular or vegetarian forms.

{ P }

Pancit canton: Chinese-style wheat noodles.

Pancit bihon: Very thin rice noodles.

Panko: Japanese coarse breadcrumbs used for crunchy deep-fried coatings. Substitute fine dry breadcrumbs.

Papaya: A tropical fruit with yellow or orange flesh and a shiny green or yellow skin. Substitute crenshaw melon to give similar color and texture but not same flavor.

Passion fruit: See LILIKO'I.

Patis: A concentrated salty brown liquid typically made from anchovies fermented in brine. Used in Southeast Asian cooking. Substitute 1 part SHOYU plus 4 parts mashed anchovies. Also called fish sauce.

Pineapple: The fruit of a bromeliad plant originally native to Brazil. It is available year-round in Hawai'i. Substitute canned pineapple.

Pipikaula: Hawaiian beef jerky.

Pipinola: Chayote plant, a member of the gourd family.

Poi: A paste made from steamed, pounded TARO. Substitute unseasoned mashed potatoes thinned to a thick batter consistency.

Poke: Hawaiian word for slice; refers to a traditional Hawaiian dish of sliced raw fish, Hawaiian salt, seaweed, and chilies.

Ponzu: Citrus-based condiment sauce made with mirin, rice vinegar, fish flakes, seaweed, and yuzu (or other citrus fruit).

Portuguese sausage: A spicy pork sausage seasoned with onions, garlic, and pepper; linguisa.

{ R }

Red chili pepper flakes: Dried and crushed red chili peppers. Substitute any chili pepper, finely chopped and seeded.

Rice wine: See SAKE.

{ S }

Saimin: Local Japanese soup made of thin wheat or egg noodles.

Sake: Slightly sweet Japanese rice wine. Substitute pale dry sherry.

Sake kasu: Leftover byproduct, called lees, when rice is turned into sake. Fermentd paste-like substance, much like miso in texture. Found refrigerated in Japanese markets near the miso.

Sambal oelek: This fiery-hot chili paste is a table condiment in Indonesia. Also known as hot Asian chili paste. Substitute any fiery-hot chili paste.

Sashimi: Very thin slices of fresh raw fish.

Sesame oil: A dense, flavorful oil pressed from SESAME SEEDS. If cold-pressed from untoasted seeds, it will be very clear and mild-flavored; if from toasted sesame seeds, it will be dark brown and strong-flavored.

Sesame seeds: Seeds of a flowering plant found throughout Eurasia and Africa with a distinctive nutty flavor. Substitute finely chopped toasted almonds.

Shallots: More like a garlic than an onion, with a head composed of one or two cloves and a mild onion flavor. Substitute green onion bulb.

Shichimi togarashi: Japanese seven flavor chili pepper mix.

Shiitake mushroom: Shiitakes have a woodsy, smoky flavor. If using the dried variety, soak in warm water for 30 minutes before using. Remove stems.

Shiso: Valued for its refreshing taste, it has beefsteak leaves. Substitute mint or basil.

Shoyu: A salty liquid made from fermented boiled soybeans, roasted barley or wheat, monosodium glutamate (MSG), and salt. Usually dark brown in color, it is the principal seasoning in Asian cooking and there are many varieties. Shoyu, the Japanese term, is the Hawai'i term for what is called SOY SAUCE on the Mainland. Substitute 3 parts Worcestershire sauce to 1 part water.

Soba noodles: Japanese buckwheat noodles, thin, and light brown in color, and eaten warm or cold. Substitute angel hair pasta.

Somen noodles: Delicate Japanese noodles made from hard wheat flour. Substitute vermicelli.

Soy sauce: See SHOYU.

Squid: When buying fresh squid, look for squid that are small and whole, with clear eyes and an ocean (but not fishy) smell. Squid must be carefully cooked so it does not become rubbery. Frequently sold as CALAMARI. Substitute octopus.

Sriracha chili sauce: U.S.-made hot sauce from sun-ripened chili peppers, vinegar, garlic, sugar, and salt. Similar to the hot sauces of Vietnam and Thailand.

Star anise: A highly fragrant dried spice that looks like a star and tastes like anise.

Sushi: A vinegar-sugar mixture rice served with raw or poached seafood, vegetables, sliced omelet, and other tasty morsels. Some sushi are wrapped in NORI.

Sweet potato: The orange-colored edible root of a tropical American vine often confused with the yam, which can be used as a substitute.

{ T }

Taro: A nutritious, starchy tuber used for making POI, the traditional Hawaiian staple. More than 200 taro varieties are grown worldwide. It cannot be eaten raw, as raw taro is full of irritating oxalic acid crystals which dissolve when boiled or steamed. Substitute any firm-fleshed potato.

Tempura: Battered and deep-fried seafood or vegetables.

Teriyaki: A marinade or sauce, generally consisting of SHOYU, sugar, GINGER, and garlic. Substitute mixture of shoyu, SAKE or sherry, sugar, and ginger.

Ti leaves: The leaves of a woody plant in the agave family grown throughout Polynesia. Used to wrap foods before cooking them in an IMU. Substitute banana leaves, corn husks, or aluminum foil.

Tobiko: Flying fish roe. Substitute any fish roe.

Tofu: Japanese name for a bland-flavored soybean curd that can be custard-like in texture (soft tofu) or quite firm. The firm and extra-firm forms are generally used in stir-frying or deep-frying.

Turbinado sugar: Pure form of cane sugar extract; light brown in color with a subtle molasses flavor. Also known as sugar in the raw. Substitute brown sugar.

{ U }

'Ulu: Hawaiian name for breadfruit.

{ W }

Wasabi: Pungent root with an extremely strong, sharp flavor. Popular Japanese HORSERADISH condiment. Substitute hot dry mustard.

Water chestnuts: An aquatic vegetable known for remaining crisp even after being cooked or canned.

Weke 'ula: Orange goatfish, often shortened to weke.

White pepper: Made from pepper berries picked when very ripe and completely red. The peppercorns are then dried. Their flavor is much milder than that of black peppercorns. Substitute black pepper.

Wok: A versatile round-bottomed pan used in Chinese cookery with and without a cover for stir-frying, steaming, boiling, braising, and deep-frying. Similar to the karhai, used in Indian cooking.

Won bok: Chinese or Napa cabbage. Substitute savoy or other green cabbage.

{ Y }

Yuzu: Japanese citrus.

Recipe Index

Following each recipe title, credit is given to the book in which the recipe originally appeared and is referenced like this:

[H] *What Hawai'i Likes to Eat*
[HH] *What Hawai'i Likes to Eat, Hana Hou*

[M] *What Maui Likes to Eat*
[BI] *What Big Island Likes to Eat*

Index

About the Authors

GAIL AINSWORTH, a Maui kama'āina and foodie has researched and written about her island for 20 years including her award-winning book *Maui Remembers: A Local History*, magazine and website articles, and three indexes to *The Maui News*.

(What Maui Likes to Eat)

BETTY SHIMABUKURO is editor of the *Honolulu Star-Advertiser's* special Wednesday *Crave* section. She has written the weekly recipe column "By Request" since 1998 whose favorites have appeared in her books *By Request: The Search for Hawai'i's Greatest Recipes* and *By Request 2: The Continuing Search for Hawai'i's Greatest Recipes*. Betty began writing about food and researching recipes after many years as a reporter.

(What Hawai'i Likes to Eat)

MURIEL MIURA earned graduate degrees in home economics education from the University of Hawai'i-Mānoa and Columbia University. She may be most recognized and known for her 1970s nationally televised cooking shows: *Cook Japanese Hawaiian Style* and *The New World of Cooking with Muriel*. She has written more than twenty cookbooks, including recently: *Japanese Cooking-Hawai'i Style, Hawai'i Cooks with Spam, Hawai'i's Party Food, What Hawai'i Likes to Eat, Homemade Gifts of Sweets and Treats, Cookies from Hawai'i's Kitchen* and *Hawai'i Cooks and Saves*. Along with Betty Shimakuro, they are the editors of Mutual's latest cookbook series, *Hawai'i Cooks*.

(What Hawai'i Likes to Eat and *What Hawai'i Likes to Eat Hana Hou)*

CHEF TYLUN PANG grew up with many cultural influences that are reflected in his style of cooking which emphasizes local farm to table ingredients. He is the Executive Chef of The Fairmont Kea Lani Maui and, as well, serves on the advisory board of the Maui Culinary Academy at the University of Hawai'i Maui College. He has received many tributes including the Mayor's Award in Culinary Excellence for County of Maui (2005), the Aipono Award for Maui County Farm Bureau's Friend of Agriculture (2012), the Aipono Lifetime Achievement Award (2014), and the Aipono Award for Best Hawai'i Regional Cuisine (2012-2016) Kō Restaurant.

(What Maui Likes to Eat)

AUDREY WILSON is a food columnist, cooking instructor, and the author of *A Mother's Gift to Her Three Sons (2007), An Eruption of Recipes from Volcano (2002),* and *Aunty Audrey's Big Island Eats (2010).* She has a weekly column for the *Hawai'i Tribune Herald* called "Let's Talk Food." She and her husband, Jim Wilson, Publisher Emeritus of the *Hawai'i Tribune Herald,* live in Volcano where they preside over AJ's Volcano Cottage, a two-unit bed and breakfast, and AJ's Volcano Cooking School.

(What the Big Island Likes to Eat)

GALYN WONG joined Mutual Publishing in 1990 as Director of Special Sales and Projects which included the research and development of cookbooks. Her culinary career began by working in numerous restaurants including New Tokyo on Beachwalk, The Willows, and Kyo-ya. Gay has become a connoisseur of island cuisine by frequently dining and studying menus at Honolulu's diverse mix of restaurants and developing a chef network.

(What Hawai'i Likes to Eat Hana Hou)